D1180275

GREENWICH LIBRARIES

3 8028 00917412 6

RACING REMINISCENCES

Racing Reminiscences

By Riders of the Past and Present.

Collected by
G. S. DAVISON
Editor of the "T.T. Special"

3

ᴥ

Another book for Motor Cyclists and all
those who believe that motor cycle road
racing is the finest sport on earth.

The T.T. Special

106, *Bristol Road, Birmingham*, 5

First printed—1948

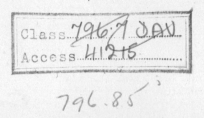

Class 796.7 DAV
Access 41215

796.85

Other books for motor cyclists :

The Story of the T.T.

The Story of the Manx.

By G. S. Davison.

KENSINGTON · PUBLIC · LIBRARIES

Made and printed in Great Britain by W. W. Curtis Ltd., Coventry

FOREWORD

IN 1930 I wrote a series of articles for the *T.T. Special* called "Racing Reminiscences." I thought at the time that this would make a good title for a book of stories, long and short, by leading riders of the past and present, and that my own might well be included.

That was over eighteen years ago—here at last is the book. And the article from which it derives its name does not appear in it !

The reason for this is that in 1942, whilst in the army, I wrote a much fuller article, not only recounting my own experiences and those of others who raced with me, but covering my own boyhood struggles and motor cycling as it was in the early 1900's. I submitted the first instalment of this to Graham Walker, who told me that it was good. Praise from such a quarter encouraged me to complete the story and, in due course, under the heading of "Forty Years On", it appeared in serial form in *Motor Cycling*.

"Forty Years On" was written not only for motor cyclists—it was intended, also, for the enlightenment of parents, particularly for parents who think that motor cycling is a dirty, dangerous game, and who forbid their sons to ride. To such sons I say—make your parents read it ; it may convert them !

Curiously enough, although that tale was written in the wilds of Northern Ireland, entirely from memory, I found when I re-read it recently, alongside the original "Racing Reminiscences," that I had missed only one episode. This described a happy evening in Belgium, more or less as follows : " . . . After we had thrown the landlord into his cellar and locked the door, Freddie and I acted as barmen and the party went merrily along. It was interrupted by the landlord who had escaped and rejoined us, breathing murder in some strange tongue . . . My last memory of that inn is of two burly members of our party sitting solidly on the landlord's stomach until the troops were safely off the premises." And with that, perhaps, I had better let memory fade, interesting as it all was at the time.

Those who read this book will find that the reminiscences of its forty-eight authors cover a wide range, from the earliest days to the present time. Several refer to the first T.T. in 1907, whilst one article—that by Mr. C. R. Collier—goes back to 1906, when the international weight limit for 1,000 cc. motor cycles was—110 lbs. ! Most of the stories, however, deal with the between-war and post-this-war periods.

The road racing " lives " of Jim Simpson and Harold Daniell will, I think, be found particularly interesting, and my thanks are due to these two great riders, and to the many others who have contributed their reminiscences ; and to the Editors of *Motor Cycling* and *The Motor Cycle* for their permission to reproduce articles of my own which appeared originally in their papers.

106, Bristol Road,   G. S. DAVISON.
    Birmingham, 5.

CONTENTS.

*Cover picture shows the late Wal Handley (A.J.S.)
in the 1929 Junior T.T.*

THIRTEENTH LUCKY

By Jim Simpson.

I rode in the T.T. every year from 1922 to 1934 inclusive, thirteen years in all; and though I made eight record or fastest laps, and was several times " placed," I never actually won until 1934—my thirteenth year in the Island.

My racing career began long before 1922, of course—in fact it may be said to have started in 1911, when I was only 13 years old. I was born in Birmingham, but when I was only a "tiddler" my parents moved to Leicester, where my father was appointed depôt manager for Rudge-Whitworths.

Rudges, if I remember rightly, produced their first motor cycle for sale to the public in 1911, and naturally my father, through selling Rudge machines, became interested in them and rode them in competitions. In fact, so did my mother! She must have been one of the very first woman trials riders, and Rudges produced a special lady's machine for her. The flat tank of those days was cut short and the top bar dropped halfway down the saddle pillar, to make it easier to ride in a skirt.

Obviously, coming from such a family it was a foregone conclusion that I should find my way on to a motor cycle, and so I did at a pretty early age. When I was 13 (without a licence, although you could get one at 14 in those days) I rode in open events such as the Doncaster speed trials and Oakamoor and Beacon hill-climbs, with a reasonable degree of success. Curiously enough it was on a Rudge, 23 years later, that I won my first T.T.

I must have weighed about 6 stone in those days, but apparently I was a coming lad! So much so, indeed, that I was actually invited to ride in the 1913 M.C.C. Inter-Team Trials when I was only about 15—and to be selected by a Club to compete in this event was quite an honour.

Then of course the war came along. Though I was really

too young, I managed to get into it, on the mechanical side, joining the M.T.A.S.C., as it was then. My job was driving a 3-ton vehicle, and I was in France from the beginning of 1916 until 1919.

When that finished we all tried to pick up the threads where we had left off, and of course my greatest ambition was to ride in the Tourist Trophy races. I joined Will Chapman, the A.J.S. distributor for Leicestershire, as a salesman and competition rider. My main idea was to try and get linked up with a reputable motor cycle manufacturer, and as Chapman was handling A.J.S. I couldn't have done better.

After a bit Will Chapman gave me a letter of introduction to the managing director of A.J.S., George Stevens, and one fine day I went over to the A.J.S. works in Wolverhampton —this was in the early part of 1920—to try and establish myself.

George Stevens was not available, but I was determined not to go away without seeing somebody who mattered, and after kicking my heels for some hours I eventually got an interview with the works manager, the late Tom Davenport (father of Leo Davenport, who won the Lightweight T.T. in 1932), and after a lot of persuasion on my part he at length agreed to employ me in the test department. This sounded very grand, but I soon discovered I was not there for the purpose of riding—oh no! My job was to sweep the floor, keep the place clean and prepare the machines for test purposes—fill them up with petrol and oil, fit sparking plugs, adjust tappets, and so on. But no chance of a ride myself!

I stuck this for a few months, earning about fifty bob a week, and presently I was able to persuade the road-test manager, Frank Giles, that I knew a bit about motor cycles and was a fairly competent type of rider. I was then permitted actually to test the machines under road conditions.

The object I had in mind all the time, of course, was to get taken on as a competition rider, but in spite of all my efforts I was never able to persuade the " works " that I was a fit and proper person to ride their machines in trials and races. I began to feel rather frustrated and disgruntled, and just about this time a friend of the family's in Leicester suggested that I should go to the Gold Coast to sell American cars to the natives and generally to run their transport. So at the end of 1920, off I went to the " Coast."

It was quite an interesting experience. I stayed there about 15 months, after which malaria and blackwater fever got me down. I came home again at the beginning of 1922 and joined Harold Petty in Leicester, which was still my home town. Harold Petty approached the Scott company, of Shipley, on my behalf, as a result of which I was entered in the 1922 Senior T.T. on a Scott. It was the very first time I had ridden in a long-distance road race of any description!

I very well remember that first crossing from Liverpool to Ramsey in the old " Fenella," and disembarking at Ramsey Pier with the Scott boys. M. Roley was the team manager, H. O. (Tim) Wood came over to look after the flock and the team consisted of Clarry Wood, Geoff Clapham, Ivor Thomas, Harry Langman and myself.

In those days riders were permitted to start practice laps from any of the " clock " stations round the course, and as the Scott team was staying at Ramsey we naturally started and finished there. I duly set off from Ramsey on my first morning, having never been round the Course before, and tried to overtake somebody on the second bend at Governor's Bridge. Result—I promptly sat on my ear! I remounted with the aid of a marshal and proceeded to the start. There they tried to stop me, because Governor's Bridge had 'phoned through to say I had been off and would the start people please see that I was O.K. to ride.

Well, I fled along to the start and motored rapidly through it, taking no notice of anybody. I got as far as Ballacraine —but here they had got a barrier across the road for me, and I had to stop! They pulled me up and read the Riot Act to me because I hadn't obeyed the signals at the start, and after

a certain amount of discussion I was able to persuade them
that I really ought to see a doctor! They hadn't got a doctor
at Ballacraine, so in the circumstances they agreed to my
going on to Kirkmichael, where there was one.

Well, obviously, all I wanted to do was to get back to
Ramsey. I did not stop at Kirkmichael, and as a result of
that escapade Tim Wood and I had to appear before Tom
Loughborough and hear the Riot Act read again. That was
my first morning's practice in the Isle of Man!

I felt very guilty for a time, for Tom had told me in no
uncertain terms what a naughty boy I was, and I decided
then that there were no medals to be won in Practice and that
the thing to do was to save everything for the race.

Race day came and there we were lined up on the starting
grid waiting for Ebby to reel off his " 5-4-3-2-1." Starting
was from cold in those days, and my Scott proved a bit obsti-
nate. By the time I really got going I was near the top of
Bray Hill and was completely out of breath! I carried on,
however, and by the time I got to Union Mills I was recover-
ing a bit. It was a beautiful day and I was beginning to
enjoy myself very much, and thinking " This is grand!"

All went well until just after Kirkmichael, when my right
foot suddenly went very cold. I couldn't account for it at
all. I thought: " This is very odd—it can't be blowing cold
on one side and hot on the other!" I waited until there was
a straight bit of road ahead, took a quick glance down, and
saw a great gush of petrol flowing over my right foot. The
bottom of the petrol tank had split, and as in those days the
Scott exhaust pipe stopped short immediately under the right
footrest I had visions of going up in smoke. I managed to
pull up without catching fire, dashed into a cottage somewhere near Bishop's Court, for a bar of yellow soap and tried
to seal the tank. It worked for a bit, but before I got to
Sulby it was doing it again, so at Ramsey I rode straight into
the garage and retired. And that was that, so far as 1922
was concerned.

In the autumn I rejoined Will Chapman of Leicester, this time on the sales and technical side, and naturally having had one go in the Isle of Man I wanted another. So I asked Chapman to do what he could for me with the Stevens brothers. The reply he got from them was to the effect that they had Howard Davies, Ossy Wade, Harry Harris and numerous others of known ability riding for them—and didn't want me! They did say, however, that if Chapman was agreeable they would let me have a ride as reserve for the works' entries. Chapman's reaction to this was: " Simpson has already competed in the T.T. If you think he's good enough to be a reserve you ought to go a bit further and give him a mount." The Stevens brothers, however, were adamant on the point, and finally Chapman said, " All right, if you won't enter him, I will. I'm not going to let him ride as a reserve but if you will build him a machine he shall ride as my entry." This was agreed to, and I represented Chapman in 1923, on a pukka job serviced by the factory.

Having failed so dismally in the 1922 race, I decided, in 1923, to make my mark during the practising period, so that if things went wrong on the race day it would at least be known that I could ride—and I think I achieved that aim. The local press referred to me as " The Leicester Flyer," and if I remember rightly I made the fastest lap that had ever been put up in practice.

I thought then, as I have ever since, that if you are to win a T.T. race the best thing to do is to lead from the start. Set a cracking pace to begin with, was my motto, and burn up as many of your competitors as possible. Then, if you are still going yourself, take things more easily in the later stages, when the engine is not feeling so good, perhaps, and you are getting a bit tired yourself. In brief, put all you know into the first three laps or so, and then see how things are going.

The first part of this procedure worked according to plan in the 1923 Junior. I set off full bore and put up a record lap from a standing start (which was allowed in those days), beating the existing record by over two minutes. I had a 23-second lead on Charlie Hough (also on an A.J.S.) and Bert le Vack (New Imperial) was third, ten seconds behind Charlie. By the end of the second lap Charlie had retired and I had increased my lead over Bert to nearly a minute and a half—though I did not know the exact amount, of course, until later.

After passing through the start at the beginning of the third lap, my idea was " one more final sprint and then take things easy." I got round Ballacraine all right and was going well as I came to the gentle " S " bend on the approach to Ballig. I went through this rather quicker than usual and when I started to pull the machine round the handlebars responded all right, but the front wheel didn't!

I came off—but I had a certain amount of control of the machine, and was only doing about 20 m.p.h. when I crashed. I picked the model up and had a look round to see what had happened; the handlebars, of course, were loose! I tightened up the centre expander pin bolt and the locking clip, and set off again. While I was working on the job Howard Davies, whom I had passed at Greeba Bridge, came by, and I said to myself, " If you can catch him by Ramsey you won't have lost too much time." Actually I came up to him at Waterworks Corner, just after Ramsey, and passed him going through the cutting.

On the next straight I found the machine a bit awkward to control—a flat back tyre. I replaced the faulty tube with a buttender and started off again. All went well to the end of the lap, but at the top of Bray Hill I suddenly came on a rider doing about 20 miles an hour, instead of 70 to 80, and using the very piece of road that I wanted myself. In those days Bray Hill was very narrow, there was a hedge each side and a definite bend at the top, so I did not see him until too late. It transpired afterwards that he had had to clap everything on to avoid a dog—it was very far from being his fault, but that didn't help me! I was travelling much too fast to pass him on the inside, but there was just a possible chance of getting by on the outside. I had a go, but my handlebars touched his, and off I came again. He was all right, for he was going so slowly, but I came a terrific box of tacks, and broke several ribs. What depressed me most was that I missed the chance of riding in the Senior. On my practice form A.J.S. had decided to offer me a mount for the Senior, but naturally I couldn't ride.

After the T.T. I rejoined A.J.S., this time as one of their official riders, and luckily my ribs were right in time for me to compete in the Ulster Grand Prix. I didn't finish, but I did manage to make the record lap for a Junior machine and only just missed making the fastest lap for the course, being beaten by one second only by Jim Whalley on a 600 Douglas.

From 1924 to 1928 I rode for A.J.S. After Howard Davies left them, at the back end of 1923, Frank Giles became their competitions manager. Frank looked after reliability trials and I took over the racing side of the team.

In 1924 I rode a " 350 " model in both Junior and Senior races—and I struck a proper packet of trouble. This was the first year A.J.S. introduced dry sump lubrication. Furthermore, they produced an engine in which the inlet valve was bigger than the exhaust. This was contrary to the accepted practice of the time, but that engine was really the forerunner of the present-day type as regards both lubrication and valve design. It was in fact a very advanced motor—perhaps a bit too advanced for its time—and with it I lapped the course at over 60 m.p.h. for the first time in the history of the race. I broke my own record lap by 2 minutes 55 seconds, at 64.54 m.p.h.—nearly a mile an hour faster than the record lap of the Senior on the following Friday—and at the end of the second lap I was leading the race by nearly 3½ minutes. Then the big inlet valve seat cracked and I packed up; but that bike was certainly a goer.

After the debacle in the Junior race the Stevens brothers decided to detune the models for the Senior to make them

" 100 per cent. safe." In spite of this I managed to get into third place on the first lap—but at nearly 2 m.p.h. less than my first lap Junior speed—and was fourth on the second and third laps. Then I broke down again, so the detuning didn't make much difference!

What we learned in 1924 had an influence, of course, on the 1925 design, and the dry sump engine was suspended—it was not, in fact, reintroduced until 1927. The 1925 engine retained the big inlet valve but in other respects it was very similar to the engine we had used in 1923. For the first time, too, a 500 c.c. engine was produced.

This year, 1925, the Stevens brothers decided it was high time they curbed my method of approach to T.T. racing. We got all our teething troubles over during practice and when it came to the start of the Junior race one would have said we had a fair chance of success. The Stevens brothers argued that the 1924 Junior had been won at 55.67 m.p.h. and that anyone who could average sixty in 1925 would have a walk-over. I argued that the record lap for 1924 had been made at nearly 65 m.p.h., about 9 m.p.h. faster than the average for the race, which had only been won at so low a speed because all the fast men broke down. I was convinced that sooner or later somebody would produce a machine which could stand all the stick the rider could give it, and that it was very far from certain that a 60 m.p.h. average would win the race. They contended that, from the design and engineering angle, no machine would stand six laps at more than sixty; therefore if I lapped regularly at 60 I should be absolutely sure of a win. The pressure on me was so great that I had to say, " All right, gentlemen, it's in your hands."

Well, that Junior race was won at 65 m.p.h. and the record lap was less than a mile an hour faster—how different from the previous year! I might well have said afterwards, " I told you so," but being an employee I had to be reasonably tactful. Freddy Dixon led off with a lap at 65½ m.p.h. from a standing start, with Wal Handley only a second behind. I myself exceeded my 60 m.p.h. schedule by lapping at just under 64, but even so I was a bad fourth. Then Freddy retired and I came up into third place. I kept on at the same speed and actually averaged 63.67 for the race, including pit stops. But Wal went streaking ahead, and won by nearly four minutes. Howard Davies was second, and although I had handsomely exceeded the " 60 m.p.h. which would be a walk-over," I had to be content with third place. So much for riding to a pre-arranged plan!

When it came to the Senior, the Stevens brothers were saying, " Look here, we did not even get the record lap in the Junior, although you finished third. What are we going to do in the Senior? You must get the record lap." I got the record lap all right, at more than 5 m.p.h. faster than the existing record, and then retired, not from mechanical failure but from an obscure electrical trouble.

In 1926 the racing policy of the firm once more became open—that is, there was no more question of the riders being controlled. But even so, I didn't have any luck. My Junior machine just wasn't fast enough and Alec Bennett, with his Velocette, went like a bomb—again a machine had been made to go quick and take all the rider could give it. I was a poor second, over ten minutes behind.

I thought I might stand a bit of a chance in the Senior, for the 500 A.J.S. was certainly a goer. But whilst the firm had had years of experience in building racing 350's, they were newcomers to the 500 class and the engine was more or less experimental. I set off full bore, led for the first two laps, and then retired—the con-rod popped out through the bottom of the crankcase. I had the satisfaction, however, of making another record lap, breaking my own Senior record of the previous year by 41 seconds and lapping the course for the first time at over seventy.

The next year—1927—saw the introduction of the chain-driven overhead camshaft model and the return of dry-sump lubrication—this time for good and all. Freddy Dixon had a run-away win in the Junior, Harold Willis was second, and I was third. My machine was never fast enough to hold Freddy, but I might have come in second if, for one thing, I hadn't hit a dog in Kirkmichael on the last lap. Right in the middle of the village there was a woman on one side of the road and a greyhound on the other. And just as I approached, the daft creature called the dog across to her. I hit it for six into a brick wall. I didn't fall off, but it slowed me a bit and affected the steering.

To make matters worse, between Parliament Square and Ramsey Hairpin the top half of the rear chain-case cover came adrift and went round with the chain! It pulled the chain off and got itself wrapped all round the sprocket. I dragged it clear without splitting the chain, pulled the chain back on to the sprocket and got going again—to finish third, only 13 seconds behind Harold Willis.

That year, however, luck was with me on the Continent. I won the Swiss Grand Prix, the German Grand Prix at the Nurburg Ring, the Austrian T.T. and the Belgian Grand Prix —the 350 class in each case—and I also won the Brooklands Grand Prix round the Mountain circuit.

For 1928 we went back to push-rods again, and after running second to Alec Bennett for three laps I lost a push-rod at Hilberry on the fourth—and wished we'd stuck to the camshaft model! In the Senior I made fastest lap and led for the first two laps, being over two minutes ahead of the next man —Joe Craig (Norton). Then I broke an exhaust valve, and that was that.

After the 1928 T.T. my long and friendly association with A.J.S. came to an end. In the past six years I had ridden in thirteen T.T. races for them—six Seniors, six Juniors and one Sidecar—and had scored one second place, two thirds and five record or fastest laps. My relationship with the firm had been a very happy one, but I thought it was about time that I had a change of ironmongery.

So I joined Nortons, who as luck would have it, after winning the 1924, '26 and '27 Seniors had just started on one of those bad patches which from time to time cross the path of all manufacturers of racing machines. My own luck was in keeping with the firm's. I retired in the 1929 Junior with a split oil tank and crashed in the Senior only four miles from the start.

Nineteen thirty, however, saw the turn of the tide. Joe Craig had come back from Northern Ireland and had rejoined the firm to look after the racing and experimental side. The whole engine had been redesigned from the word " go " and was a real sound job, although in the T.T. it was just not fast enough to hold the Rudges, which were having a year " in." As everyone knows, Wal Handley won the Senior in magnificent style, with Graham Walker on another Rudge second. I was third, 4½ minutes behind Wal.

The basis of that 1930 " 500 " engine was 100 per cent. sound and solid, and after the T.T. the firm got down to the job of providing just a bit more of the necessary urge. The result was that we finished off the season in fine style. Stanley Woods won the Ulster Grand Prix and the French Grand Prix, in which latter event I made record lap at 84.63 m.p.h Tim Hunt won the Spanish T.T., I think, and I myself collected the Swedish Grand Prix. By now we had got both reliability and speed.

Unfortunately I had a nasty crash in the French Grand Prix at the end of the season. I was batting along at about 105 during early morning practising on a long straight, and in the distance I saw some people standing at the side of the road. As I drew nearer I noticed that the group was composed of several gendarmes and a civilian. I found out later that the civilian was a local farmer who wanted to cross the road. The gendarmes were apparently telling him that he couldn't do so until practising was finished, and he was having a great argument with them. In the heat of this argument they had forgotten there was actually anybody coming along the road until they heard me arriving. The moment their attention was distracted the civilian, with his bicycle, set off to cross the road. I saw this happening and steered to go behind him, but he looked up, saw me coming, changed his mind and started to go back. I hit him, of course, and he was very badly knocked about—he died later in hospital. I also went into hospital, with three fractures in the left leg three in the left hand, and scars on my face which are there to-day. I was entirely exonerated from blame, both by the police and by the unfortunate man's relatives, who came round to apologise and to commiserate with me.

That was the end of racing for me that year.

Now we come to 1931. I think this was the first year that four laps had been done during a morning practice period. I did it myself with a Junior machine, and it meant lapping at an average of under 30 minutes, which was pretty quick for those days—they were record practice laps. I did it, though, as a consumption test rather than a speed test. We were most anxious to do a one-fill race of seven laps and these practice laps proved that it could be done.

In the 1931 Junior we were given definite riding instructions—for the first time since those far-off days when the Stevens brothers had told me to average sixty and no more. But they were very different instructions—this is how it was.

On practice form it seemed a certainty that the four official Norton riders—Jim Guthrie, Tim Hunt, myself and Stanley Woods (to put us in alphabetical order)—would finish one—two—three—four. Mr. Bill Mansell, Norton's gaffer, very reasonably argued that if we were to race it out between our selves we might blow up and spoil the firm's chances. But there was no business of drawing lots, or anything of that sort. Mr. Mansell laid it down that whoever led at the end of the first lap was to keep that position and the other three would be signalled to keep in their respective places. In other words, it was to be an open race between us for one lap and we were then to be controlled. Nobody could have asked for a fairer arrangement than that—but, as often happens, things didn't go according to plan.

Well, on the first lap I led by 16 seconds, Stanley Woods being second. Freddie Hicks on the A.J.S. was third, Ernie Nott (Rudge) fourth and Jim Guthrie fifth. Tim Hunt had had a short stop and wasn't on the leader board.

Anyway, I was leading, and in due course I got the appropriate signal. By the end of the third lap I was just over half a minute ahead of Stanley, Freddie Hicks had retired, leaving Ernie Nott in third place, with Nortons' other two men, Guthrie and Hunt, fourth and fifth. But in the fourth lap Stanley slowed down, and Tim broke the lap record and came into second place only 23 seconds behind me.

Now Tim was No. 3 and I was No. 23—and we were riding at half-minute intervals. So it was easy for our pit manager to see how we lay. And at the end of the fifth lap I was very much surprised to get a signal telling me that I was now running second, 14 seconds behind Tim—not at all according to plan.

" What's going on here?" I thought—and set off full bore to try and pick up those 14 seconds, and some more as well. And then, at the Mountain Gate after the Bungalow — my engine cut clean out. I checked things over—there was no indication of a plug whiskering or oiling, no sign of misfiring or petrol starvation, no mechanical noises. I had been so accustomed to engine failures in the past that the moment it happened I kicked the gear into neutral and decided to coast on towards the Start. Then at Windy Corner I saw Jack Lawrence, a director of Nortons. He held out a bottle of Worthington to me—and I just couldn't pass it! I pulled up. Jack said, " What's wrong?" I said " . . . . . ", and drank the Worthington.

After that I decided to do a bit more investigation. I pulled the bike on to the stand, put it in top gear and felt the compression—the compression was there, the engine turned over all right. I took the end cover off the magneto armature,

saw that the make-and-break was all right, plug was O.K.,
no signs of heating or white metal. I put a new plug in and
tried again—still it wouldn't start. I hauled it back on the
stand once more and checked the carburetter—yes, the float
chamber flooded all right, the petrol was there. What the
devil——?

Why I did it I don't know, but I decided to open the
throttle fully, go on flooding the carburetter and see if petrol
came up the needle jet. It didn't. The main jet had a bayonet
type fixing; I whipped it out—and the mystery was solved!
There was a piece of enamel in the jet! I cleared it, put the
jet back, started off again—and finished eighth.

That was the Junior race in 1931: now we come to the
Senior.

When we were having a quiet drink in the Castle Mona on
the Thursday night I said to Mr. Mansell, " What do we do
to-morrow?" " After Monday," he replied, " you can please
yourselves. I'm not going to try to control you, one way or
the other. If you can win, get on with it, and good luck to
you!" So we had no riding instructions on the Friday.

I was second on the first lap—Jim Guthrie was ahead of
me by exactly one second. On the second lap I took the lead
and on the third I was well in front, having created a lap
record of over 80 for the first time. And strange as it may
seem, this was on a lap which included running out of petrol
at Governor's Bridge! I managed to coast up out of the hol-
low, and the engine picked up again, gave a couple of
splutters and just got me to the pits.

I refuelled, set off on the fourth lap and came unstuck at
Ballaugh Bridge—and not because I was going too quickly.
This was just one of those things the T.T. teaches us. My
record lap was over 4½ m.p.h. up on that of the previous year
and 4 m.p.h. faster than anything Nortons had done in practice. Those three strenuous opening laps of mine had played
hell with the brake linings, which were beginning to get a bit
sticky. The front brake grabbed at Ballaugh Bridge and

fetched me off. Result—out of the race when leading by over a minute and a half on the third lap, and a couple of broken ribs.

My luck was mixed again for the next two years—1932 and '33. I got record Senior lap once more in 1932, this time at 81.5 m.p.h, but after leading for the first two laps dropped back and had to be content with third place at the end. Part of the trouble was again the front brake—approaching Cregny-baa on the fifth lap the cable broke. This time, fortunately, I did not come off.

More trouble in 1933. In the Junior race I packed up at Ballaugh in the last lap, when running third, and in the Senior I finished second, a minute and a half behind Stanley Woods, having covered the last five laps without a clutch! I was getting used to being known as "Unlucky Jim."

But 1934 put paid to that. In the Junior I had a grand race with my team-mate, Jim Guthrie. He led throughout and I was second throughout, but it was a close thing. Jimmy G. was two seconds ahead of me on the first lap, ten seconds in the next and sixteen seconds on the third. He did a very quick fourth lap—half a minute, nearly, better than the average of his first three, whereas mine was slightly slower than my average, so when he came in to re-fuel at the end of the fourth he was a full minute ahead.

On the fifth lap I was faster than Jimmy G., and got to within eight seconds of him; but it was ten seconds on lap 6 and nine on the seventh and last. A fine race for both of us, though, with the third man nearly six minutes away.

That was the first day of my last T.T. week, for I had decided several months before that I would pack it in after the end of the 1934 season. At the back end of 1933 I had joined the Shell company. I was thirty five, I had had thirteen years of it, and I was beginning to think that it was time I stopped. I persuaded the Shell company to let me ride for one more year and promised them that I wouldn't ask again. So it was a coincidence that I won a T.T. race on my

last year's racing—I didn't just go on until I won, as some
people seem to think. And it was a coincidence that it was
the luckiest year I ever had!

Twenty three years after I had first ridden Rudges in local
speed trials and hill-climbs, I was back in the saddle of a
Rudge for the 1934 Lightweight. And a fine little machine it
was. I made fastest lap, took the lead on the third lap and
held it to the end—just the opposite of what I had so often
done, that is, take the lead at the beginning and fade out
of the picture before the end!

In the Senior, my last T.T. race, luck was with me again.
I hadn't got the urge to win, and was, in fact, a fairly bad
third all the way through the race until the last lap. And
then, when only a few miles from home, Stanley Woods, who
was lying second on a Husqvarna, ran out of petrol and let
me into his place. In my twelve previous T.T. years I had
scored two second and four thirds but never more than one
" place " in any one year; in my thirteenth, lucky year I
scored two seconds and a win. And to sugar it, so to speak
followed on by winning the Junior class of the Dutch T.T.
and the Belgian, German, Swedish and Ulster Grand Prix,
and both Junior and Senior of the " Swiss."

I have often been asked if, after so many eventful years of
racing, it were not an awful wrench to give it up. Very definitely, the answer is " No." For one thing I had made the
decision some months before; for another, I realised that I
had had enough. The game was still as fine as ever, but for
me the " kick " had gone out of it. I had enjoyed it immensely, but I gave it up without any effort at all. It's a
mistake to go on too long and when, as Noel Coward says,
" the thrill has gone, to linger on will spoil it anyhow."

So fourteen years ago I gave it up. Since then I have seen
every T.T. race and I'm never going to miss one—even if I
have to be taken over to the Island in a bath chair.

I cannot end this story without paying tribute to two of
the most brilliant riders the world has ever seen—Wal

Handley and Jim Guthrie. They seldom raced against each other, for Wal scored the last of his successes the same year that Jimmy G. scored the first of his—1930. But they had in common a spirit that knows no defeat. Unlike some other fine riders who, throughout a race have always looked like winning, and have won with apparent confidence and ease, Walter and Jimmy were often up against something, battling grimly, even furiously with unexpected packets of trouble. And the greater the difficulties, the more dogged they became. The race of the moment was the one thing that mattered— there was no thought of the future, no count of the risk. In the days of Nelson one would have said that they raced " For Death or Glory " and even in these prosaic times I can find no better words to describe them. They were two of the grandest chaps on earth.

I SCARED 'EM STIFF
By Stanley Woods.

A short story about my T.T experiences is rather a difficult assignment. Most of the stories I can think of are either too long or unprintable! To one who took the game as seriously as I, the humorous side seldom appeared, or if it did it was definitely unfit for publication. But in 1935 there occurred an incident which even now makes me chuckle when I think of it.

One typical practice morning, when the mantle of Mona lay heavily on the shoulders of Snaefell, a rider, not very familiar with the course, ran out of road on the left bend about half a mile after the East Mountain Gate.

He was not travelling fast enough to be hurt and as he picked himself up and attempted to sort out the damage he was joined, almost without warning, by another rider.

While commiserating with, or cursing, each other, they became aware of the approach of yet a third rider. But, while the first had run out of road in a gentle sort of manner and the second had just quietly dropped in without any fuss at all, the approaching rider, judging by the roar of his exhaust, was about to annihilate himself and all in his path.

Spellbound, they listened for a couple of seconds. Then, abandoning their bikes to their fate in the gutter, they scrambled away up the Mountain, intent on getting clear.

The noise was from the exhaust of my Senior Moto Guzzi. Visibility was so poor that I was not really hurrying myself, and having passed the East Mountain Gate in a thick bank of mist, I remained in second gear—which gave me a speed of 85 m.p.h. at peak revs.—until I got clear of the thickest bank of cloud.

Cracking along at or near peak revs. in second, I must have been making quite a noise, and with visibility reduced to eight or ten yards it must have appeared to the two lads in trouble that whoever was approaching through the mist was heading for certain trouble.

At any rate, as I rounded the bend I caught a glimpse of two shadowy figures scrambling madly up the Mountain, and was rather puzzled to account for their actions.

On completing the lap I pulled into the Paddock, for, with visibility so poor, practising was, for me, a waste of time. Over a cup of cocoa I was amusing some of the lads with the tale of the riders turned hikers, when they arrived, and seemed quite peeved at the way I had scared them!

THAT LAP AT " 91 "
BY HAROLD DANIELL.

I have often been asked how I made that record lap in 1938 and I have usually answered that I haven't the slightest idea! Now, at last, I will try to explain how it came about.

Well, first of all, I have always found that I tend to go quicker towards the end of a race than in the early stages. Perhaps it is that I am a bad starter, and that I sort of " wind up " as the race goes on and I get used to things. At any rate, I seem to increase my speed, lap by lap, and in practically every race that I've finished, my last lap has been my best—and this goes right back to the Manx Grand Prix of 1933. Perhaps it's getting settled in that does it. Conversely, whenever I go full bore at the beginning of a race I seem to break down—that's happened on several occasions.

I think that record laps—certainly insofar as they apply to me—are made by driving the model really hard—almost over-driving it, in fact—rather than by taking corners dangerously fast. Ultra-fast cornering, particularly in a long race, is not worth the risk and to my mind does not really save any appreciable time. It is quite different, of course, on a short circuit, for the style of riding there is different, and that's why, I think, chaps who are brilliant on a short circuit sometimes don't show up so well in the Isle of Man. I don't regard Donington as a short circuit, of course.

About this over-driving. Every rider in a works' team is told the " maximum permissible revs." of his engine and if he exceeds these revs., he is asking for trouble. Usually he keeps two or three hundred r.p.m. below them—I do, as a rule, anyway, and I certainly did in the 1938 Senior.

I can't remember the exact gear ratio or the maximum permissible revs. of my 1938 Norton, but the ratio was somehow in the region of 4½ to 1 and the " maximum " about 6500. For the first four laps I kept down to about 6200. Now the Norton in the top gear was capable of just over the 120 mark. Third gear was 10 per cent. lower, only—say 4.95 to 1 and in that gear at 6500 I could do 115. But 6200 in third means less than 110—and what a difference that little extra can make on the many long rises of the T.T. course when one can either be careful of the engine in top, or cane it in third.

Now to the 1938 Senior. I started off carefully, for I had had trouble early in the Monday's Junior when I gave it the gun right from the start. I used full throttle, of course, as soon as the motor was warmed up, but I kept the revs. well below maximum. For the first three laps I averaged 88.20 m.p.h. against Stanley Woods' 88.82 and was 32 seconds

behind him, with Freddy Frith lying second in between us.
My laps had been done in 26.1, 25.42 and 25.19 respectively.
When I stopped to refuel at the end of the third lap I was told
I was a good half minute behind Stanley and that " I had
better do something about it." I had a quick fill-up, which
saved me several seconds, and then I started to stir the bicycle up a bit. My fourth lap, including the pit stop, took
25.54, which wasn't so bad.

The end of the fourth lap was really the turning point for
me. My fifth lap took 25.5—just over the 90 mark—and I
was really driving the model. We went better still in the sixth
lap, and though I didn't know it until later, of course, beat
the 25 minutes for the first time, with a lap in 24.57. At the
end of the sixth lap I was given the signal " 1 + 4," which
meant that I was leading by four seconds. I didn't know that
I had beaten the lap record, and I certainly didn't intention-
ally " go " for it on the last lap. But that pit signal had
shown me that it was bound to be a very close thing and I
just went on driving the machine up to the " maximum permissible revs," with the result that my last lap was the fastest
of the day—24 minutes 52 3/5th secs. at exactly 91 miles an
hour. And, believe it or not, I took no more risks on that lap
than on any other.

One thing that counts a lot, of course, is the weight of the
machine towards the end of a race, when the tank is getting
empty. Our tanks that year held approximately five gallons
of petrol and we could just do four laps on a full tank—
actually I found later that I finished with so little petrol in
the tank that there was scarcely enough to provide a sample
for the examiners! Now petrol weighs approximately eight
pounds a gallon, so five gallons weigh forty pounds. In other
words, on a four lap run the machine gets ten pounds lighter
on each lap, and the important thing is that this weight reduction takes place at the top of the bicycle. So you not only get
a lighter machine with better acceleration and braking, but
you get a model which handles much better as well.

All in all, therefore, it is only reasonable that the last lap should be your best, provided that the model is functioning O.K. and that you are not getting tired.

FRANCORCHAMPS FROLICS

By Tyrell Smith.

One race which stands out in my rapidly failing memory rather more than most, is the Belgian Grand Prix of 1930.

The 500 class promised to be a real " do," and very shortly after the start, the leading group resolved itself into Woods and Simpson (Nortons), Handley (F.N.), Dodsen (Sunbeam), Duncan (Raleigh), Jimmy Guthrie (A.J.S.) and Uncle Graham Walker and yours truly on Rudges. Those first few laps were hectic in the extreme, as the speed of these particular machines varied by only one or two m.p.h. The actual leadership kept constantly changing, and the bumping and boring was nobody's business. Jimmy Guthrie's A.J.S. appeared to be the slowest of the bunch, but what it lacked in speed was more than made up for by Jim's exuberance.

Round about the second lap, I managed to draw ahead of Jim on the run down the Masta straight, round poor old Bill Hollowell's corner, and was nicely aimed into the Stavelot hairpin with the brakes hard on. Suddenly that uncanny sixth sense warned me that all was not as well as it should have been, and I straightened up a little and did not lay the old Rudge into the hairpin as I had intended to. Lucky I did so, as Jim and the A.J.S. shot across my front wheel at an incredible velocity. I don't know whether Jim was leading the A.J.S. or vice versa, but both disappeared in the direction of Stavelot village in a shower of dust and small stones! Safely round the hairpin, I had a peep back whilst the revs were building up in first, and was relieved to see a somewhat disgruntled Jim preparing to push off.

The pace of the first few laps soon began to tell, and some of the faster machines fell by the wayside. This made the way a bit easier for those still battling for the lead, but to keep the excitement up, Jimmy Guthrie was very shortly once again amongst those present.

I should mention here that at this time no alterations had taken place at the Eau Rouge corner. One came pretty rapidly downhill past the Tribunes, round a sharpish left hand bend with a deep ditch at the outside and then round a wide uphill right handed hairpin, with a rather loose gravelly surface. From here the road straightened out, and then curved up and to the left, to climb along the outside of a hill. This meant, of course, that there was a steep grassy downhill slope on the outside of the road.

About quarter distance, the same little party, now slightly reduced in numbers, was still fighting it out, and Jim and I were still in close company, past the Tribunes and around the Eau Rouge hairpin, Jim in the lead. He gave the Ajay all it had, got away from the hairpin, and in those pre-magaphone days the 500's had some quite useful urge at the bottom end, especially on a loose surface.

Rounding the left hand bend up the hill, the A.J.S. began to slide, but Jim grimly kept the throttle wide open, hoping, no doubt, that the grass verge would stop the slide. However, he must have left one of his mascots on the mantelpiece that day, for first over went the Ajay, and the last I saw of Jim were the soles of his boots, vanishing rapidly down the hillside.

The two Sunbeams, Dodson in front and Simcock behind, appeared to be the stiffest opposition to the Rudges, and about halfway through the race I drew up alongside Graham to discuss our tactics. This " conference " took place on the comparatively straight uphill run from Stavelot towards Francorchamps. Whilst engaged in converse, and riding six inches apart at 90 odd, we rapidly drew up on some unfortunate foreigner, all knees, elbows and backside, complete with hot-cross bun crash hat, doing his utmost to coax the fifty-ninth m.p.h. out of a somewhat seedy 175 two stroke. Graham and I parted just sufficiently to clear our friend, Graham passing on the outside, me on the inside. After passing, something prompted us both to look back, when we beheld the spectacle of palsy-walsy, standing up on the footrests, a most agonized expression on his face, in the throes of a full-lock wobble. I am afraid we did not improve his friendly feelings towards the British!

To save the race from getting too monotonous, Fate had still one alarum in store for me. In the heat of the afternoon, and the closing laps of the race, feeling somewhat jaded, my old Rudge cracking as well as ever, we commenced the left hand downhill swoop towards Burnenville. I had been closing up on No. 8, an ample Dutchman mounted on a Rudge, when I realised with horror, that, instead of sticking to the right hand side of the road, he intended cutting over to the left, although travelling 40 m.p.h. too slowly to justify such a manoeuvre.

I could not possibly pull the Rudge over to get inside him, so I just laid it over, and trod well and truly on the brake. The model went into a glorious full lock broadside—we were travelling at round about the 100—my front wheel just missing his back wheel, but rushing dangerously close towards the right hand back. I became suddenly conscious that I was not alone, and a lightning glance to port revealed Digger Simcock on his 350 " Beam," also broadsiding, about a foot from my left hand handlebar grip. He must have been right on my tail, and had to execute the same manoeuvre to miss me, as I had to do to miss the Dutchman! However, our two models righted themselves, and we went on our way rejoicing, but, as far as I was concerned, paying a little more attention.

Justice is said to be poetic. With but two or three laps to go, and having just been given the griffin that I was in the lead, I came up once again upon No. 8 just past the Tribunes. He took the left hand bend at the bottom at an impossibly

high speed, no doubt trying to make up for the lack of knots
in his over-burdened Rudge, and disappeared into the afore-
mentioned deep ditch, the last I saw of him being a descend-
ing cascade of muddy water.

Who says racing isn't fun?

SWEDISH EXERCISES
By Geoff Davison.

One Monday morning many years ago, when I was sitting
at my desk writing a technical article, the telephone bell rang
—and thereby hangs this tale.

" Hello, is that you, Davy?" said a Voice. " This is
Henry speaking. Will you ride for us in the Swedish T.T.
next week-end? I'd entered Johnson, but he's ill."

" Why pick on me?" I replied. " I'm no good these
days."

" Good God, I know that," said the Voice, with what I
thought unnecessary candour. " And if there was anyone
else with two legs and two arms who'd go I wouldn't ask you.
But Johnson can't possibly be well in time and everyone else
who can ride at all is in the big race at Brocklands on Saturday." He continued, a little less irritably. " So if you can't
do it, I'll have to scratch the entry. What d'you say?"

" I'll have a crack," I answered, " but you know I've
never ridden one of your jobs and ——"

" Oh I know you won't do any ruddy *good*," said the
Voice, getting a little edgy again, " but I've paid for the
entry and the insurance and I might as well get a run for my
money. You can have William as a mechanic."

" Why William?" I asked. " He's stone deaf. Does he
speak Swedish?"

" Of course he doesn't ruddy well speak Swedish," snorted
the Voice. " And what the hell does it matter if he's deaf
so long as he can fill you up with petrol and adjust the chains
—d'you want to make love to him?"

" No," I replied with a shudder; I knew William. " But anyway—what sort of course is it—how long—what about gear ratios . . . ?"

" I don't know a damned thing about it," said the Voice, and I could almost feel its blood-pressure rising. " You'll find out when you get there. The point is: are you on?"

" Expenses?" I asked.

" Just about," said the Voice. " And anything you can pick up is yours. Meet William at the station at three o'clock to-morrow. And don't forget your crash-helmet. Judging by what I saw of you in the T.T., you'll need it."

This frank and pleasant conversation then ended, and I did some swift telephoning to the Barons. The results were poor. The Barons, like the Voice, knew little about the Swedish T.T. and cared less.

Three days later William and I landed at Gothenburg complete with a natty little racer in full T.T. trim and a bagful of chains and sprockets. We were met by the local agent for the make and whistled along to a powerful hotel where a reception appeared to have been arranged for us. The Voice had done his advance publicity well. Indeed hospitality, I thought.

For an hour or more we ate, drank and chatted. There were about twenty of us in the room and most of them were local pressmen; all spoke excellent English. Apparently I was the first Englishman to compete in the Swedish T.T., and I was the evening's Big Story. Presently they began to filter away, and at last there were only four of us left, William and I, the agent and the head waiter—who presented us with the bill! Hospitality?—well, we got a very good press next day! Armed with sheaves of newspapers which I gathered told Sweden what a wonderful rider I was, we set off for the course.

And what a course! So far as I remember it was about four miles round, was in most places about six feet wide and was everywhere several inches deep in dust and stones. (I believe that a new course was found in subsequent years, but I never went there again—once was enough!) The total length of the race was about 40 miles, so a dirt-track type tank would have done; my tank held over three gallons A top gear of about 8 to 1 would have been ideal; with all my sprockets I could not get below 6, and never once did I get into top gear. As a timed section in a reliability trial that course would have been quite interesting, but as a race circuit—especially with dozens of vast Husqvarnas on it, whose riders seemed to find their way by instinct through the dust-clouds and to know the location of every concealed boulder —it was not my cup of tea at all.

The race was even worse than the practising, for it was held late in the afternoon and the sinking sun, seen through the dust screen, turned the atmosphere into a sort of blood-red nightmare, like pictures of Mount Etna in eruption. Mainly in bottom gear, with occasional bursts in second, blinded, suffocated and all but unconscious, I tottered round and round. Almost everyone fell off and in the end I finished second in my class—yes, and there were three finishers!

The result could not have been more satisfactory—a Swedish rider first, the gallant(?) English visitor second; a terrific banquet followed. William and I reached it about 8 p.m. and the buffet part of it was then in full swing. We ate and drank and drank and ate; and drank; and drank and ate again. During a lull they presented the prizes, of which I seemed to collect an undue share. The winner, so far as I could gather, was awarded a cup. For being second I was presented with a cup, a plaque, a medal and god-knows-what-else.

Up to that time we had been, so to speak, in the snack-bar department only, for after the prize distribution we found ourselves at tables for the orgy proper. William and I, honoured guests, were at opposite ends of the top table, with all the dooks and earls and nobby parties—and, I may say, their daughters and so-ons. And what daughters—all the most perfect, hand-picked blondes. There were about thirty of us at our table, with the sexes evenly distributed. So you will gather, by simple arithmetic, that William and I each hand a beautiful hand-picked blonde on each side of us. What made it more palatable to me was the fact that they all spoke perfect English and were well abreast of the times.

William, of course, though equally well placed, physically, was handicapped by the fact that being stone deaf he could not hear what his beautiful neighbours were saying and had similarly no idea that they could understand him. He sat there, absorbing what was placed before him, and surveying the blondes with an appraising eye. I had a feeling that something dreadful might happen at any moment. It did.

Suddenly, across the acres of table, came these terrible words:

" Davy," roared William, " I reckon these Swedish tarts are a bit of ruddy all right. If I don't click with one to-night I'll go crackers."

There was an " Orrible Ush " as the words sank in. Flushes mounted to the cheeks of the beautiful blondes. The hush was then replaced by a confused chatter—I couldn't understand a word of it, but it was clear that everyone was quickly " talking of something else."

My nerve had gone. Nothing, even in that hectic race, had been so terrifying as this· It was about midnight. Making some incoherent excuse, I gathered my trophies, fled from the room and caught the 1 a.m. train. I didn't give a damn what happened to William.

SNAGS AT SIGNPOST

By Bert Kershaw.

Most—or at any rate many—of my T.T. troubles seem to have occurred at Signpost Corner.

One day during the 1921 Practices, when I was riding a 250 New Imperial, I was coming round Signpost Corner when, without the slightest warning, the right handle-bar broke clean off at the stem lug. I trickled back to the garage, fitted a new pair of handlebars, and forgot all about the incident.

Then came the Lightweight Race. I was doing very nicely, thank you, at half distance—it was a five lap race in those days—and was actually leading the race by about three minutes, with Doug Prentice on another New Imp about three minutes behind. Then, at Signpost Corner on the third lap—my right handlebar broke off again. I clipped the carburettor controls on to the left bar and continued to the pits, where I had to retire. That was the nearest I ever got to winning a T.T. race!

But Signpost Corner still had a down on me. Three years later, in the Junior, I was going round it on a Barr and Stroud with outside flywheel—when the flywheel flew off! The sprocket was still intact but the old B. & S. didn't go so well without a flywheel, so I packed it in again.

Beware of Signpost Corner; like the elephant, it never forgets!

HISTORIC PILE-UP
By Les Martin.

The most amazing spectacle I ever saw, or ever expect to see, as a rider, occurred in the first lap of the 1934 Ulster Grand Prix, when Jimmy Guthrie's slip off the road resulted in a most terrific pile-up.

I followed Ernie Nott off the mark in the 250 class, two minutes after the 500's and with the 350's sandwiched in between—massed start, of course—and when approaching the second left-hander from the start, and just getting into my stride, I noticed the blue flag (at that time used as a danger signal) being waved frantically by a marshall on the bank.

Before Ernie or I could do more than shut the throttle, we were in the middle of this full-bore bend, and there confronting us, not much more than 50 yards up the road (and

occupying most of it) one could see about six or eight machines on the ground, a pyramid of dust rising from them and
riders hopping off and allowing their machines to join the
pile.

Subsequently there were, I believe, fourteen machines down
altogether, and I think Ernie and I went through what gap
was left with less than a foot to spare. I know Ginger Wood's
big twin New Imperial was on our right, spinning round on
one footrest, and a lot of the machines were roaring their
hearts out on a fair amount of throttle, and riders seemed to
be mixed up with them.

I have ridden in every Ulster since then, and lots of other
races, but I shall never forget that '34 pile-up. Strange to
relate, I can't remember ever reading a report about it—and,
stranger still, although I for one was wondering for the rest
of the race how many riders had been killed, not one of them
was even seriously hurt!

SO NEAR AND YET SO FAR
By ERNIE NOTT.

The best fun I have had in any race, followed by the most
disappointing finish, was the 1931 Lightweight T.T., for I
could certainly have won it, I think, if I had had a couple of
sixpenny spanners with me!

I was riding a Rudge, along with Graham Walker and
Tyrell Smith. These machines had proved so fast and reliable—one of us seemed bound to win—that we thought it
unnecessary to carry pocketsful of tools around with us. So as
regards tools, I was travelling light.

When race day came along, our Rudges soon showed that
there was nothing to touch them. On the first lap I led
Tyrell by three quarters of a minute with Graham a few
seconds behind Tyrell. Same order the second lap. On the
third lap Graham overhauled Tyrell, but my own lead on
him was two and three-quarter minutes, which I increased
to nearly four minutes by the fifth and sixth laps.

And then, on the mountain in the last lap, the locking nut on the inlet tappet came unput. I fiddled around with it and got going again—but oh for a pair of tappet spanners! Right to the finish I had to hold the tappet rod in position with my hand—a difficult and painful job—and to make matters worse, trying to get round Governor's Bridge steering single handed, I fell off! Up again and so to the finish, in fourth place ten minutes behind Graham whom I had been leading by four minutes a few miles back.

So near and yet so far? Or so far—and so near?

LYONS IN CAPTIVITY

By Ernie Lyons.

For an amusing incident, what about the following? It happened at the Cookstown 100 in Northern Ireland in 1938. I was riding my Speed Twin from, as far as I can remember, the scratch mark. As some of the early starters had almost 30 minutes start on me I was not in any hurry about leaving the " paddock," which in this instance was the market yard at Cookstown. When the race had been in progress perhaps 20-25 minutes I decided to take my place on the line—engine nicely warm from riding round the yard, goggles ready polished. Imagine my consternation when it was discovered that the gates had been locked and nobody seemed to know who had the key! There was a terrific to-do, but the key was eventually discovered in time to get me on to the line before the flag fell.

And what a race! A dusty, untarred road little better than a laneway formed one leg of the course, with conveniently open gates (and were they used!) at the more dangerous bends. As a contrast, the course then passed along the main street of Cookstown—one of the widest streets in the British Isles!

DICING WITH DENIS

By Eric Briggs.

The two most interesting rides I have had in the I.O.M. were the Junior and Senior Manx, 1947. Both were similar, i.e. in both I was chasing Denis Parkinson who started one minute in front of me in each race. In the Junior I caught him on the second lap at the Mountain Box. He repassed me in the mist near Windy and I passed him immediately after Creg-ny-Baa. At the pit stop he filled quicker than I, because, by a misunderstanding, I pulled into the wrong pit. The chase began all over again, and I caught and passed him at the Mountain Box once more!

In the Senior things were a little closer, and I did not see him until I was approaching the Gooseneck on the last lap. By the time the Bungalow was reached I was on his tail and ready to pass him, but as it was then raining heavily and the roads were greasy I decided that being so near the finish and having a good lead there was no point in " dicing " and risking us both coming off! So I stayed behind, content in the knowledge that I had at least caught him up on the road.

THE LADY CLAIMED DAMAGES

By Len Horton.

On the approach to Sulby Bridge in the 1925 Junior, I think it was, I was overtaking a rider when I felt petrol coming into my face. As I drew level I looked at his machine and saw petrol streaming from his carburetter, so while riding side by side I yelled at him and jabbed my finger at his carburetter.

It was very difficult to make him understand what was happening, and when I looked ahead again I was rather closer to the bridge corner than was good for me, with absolutely no hope of taking it. I went instead for the rope across the opening on the left, and managed to negotiate that safely— I don't quite know how. But the next thing I met was an Orange Cart. This I didn't negotiate, but knocked it clean over, which made a bit of a mess. I bounced off the cart and knocked over a few people.

I did not realize this at the time, being in a great hurry, but picked up the bike, got back on the road (I had to have the rope lifted considerably to do this, although I had negotiated it quite successfully going the other way!), straightened the handlebars and footrests as much as possible, took a run and was away again.

I had not gone far before I discovered that I had lost the complete sole off my boot.

The sequel to this story is that a few days later when I was back at the works, the managing director received a letter from a girl who said that she had been knocked down with others at Sulby Bridge and that various articles of clothing had been scrapped. She would be very pleased if we could send her—and here followed a list something like this:

> 1 Frock
> 1 Pr. Stockings
> 1 Pr. Knickers
> 1 Pr. Corsets

and so on (Eh? Ed.). But she was very sporting, and said that if supplying these would get the marvellous rider who had joined them at Sulby for a short time into trouble, she would not claim them. Naturally, the things were sent along, the managing director's typist going out and buying them.

The petrol-spraying rider, by the way, was Charles Hough, whom I passed a little farther on, out of petrol.

RACING AT THIRTEEN YEARS OLD
By Denis Parkinson.

The outstanding memories of my racing career are my first season in Grass Track racing, at the age of 13, and the winning of the Lightweight M.G.P. for the third successive year.

When I was only twelve years old my father bought me a 147 c.c. Rex Acme Villiers, on which I used to tear round a field where our local Club boys practised for their Grass Track events—and I could really buzz this wee model around. In 1929, when I was 13, the Wakefield Club held a Grass Track Race Meeting at Ossett, Yorks., and the Club people thought it would be quite a novelty for me to take part in the racing. I did so, and enjoyed myself thoroughly: I wanted more!

So for the rest of 1929 I visited Grass Tracks at Tadcaster, York, Ingbirchworth, Harrogate and Dewsbury, and won no fewer than five cups before reaching the age of 14. The organisers of these various meetings used to take one look at me in short pants, and the wee 147 model, and my handicap was just the job. By not trying too hard in the heats and semi-finals, and maintaining my handicap till the final, I got away with it. Mind you, I never got away with it twice at the same meeting! They were very happy memories, and my most treasured picture in my scrap book is one taken "at speed " at one of these meetings.

This early start stood me in good stead for later years, and it may be remembered that I was only 21 when I won my first Lightweight M.G.P. in 1936.

The second outstanding episode was in the 1938 Lightweight Manx, when I hoped to pull off a triple win by collecting the Trophy for the third time running. In practice, the late Alan Worswick broke the existing 250 Manx lap record on three different mornings. Worswick, always an early starter, would go out and wallop the record and then I, following on, would knock a few seconds off his newly established time. In fact, as the records will show, I got in a practice lap as low as 30 m. 7 sec., which is not bad for a British 250 c.c. model.

Unfortunately, wind spoilt any chance of getting near this on race day, but after lying second to Worswick, only one second behind, on the first lap, I broke the lap record on the second lap, which put me in the lead, and there I stayed to the end. (Incidentally, that lap record of mine still stands). And what a thrill I experienced on the last ride down to the finish from Governor's Bridge! Quite my proudest moment.

A SWISS EPISODE
By Bill Beevers.

I was one of the only two English competitors in the 1946 Geneva Grand Prix. Each of us was offered a gold wrist watch if either of us finished, the donor being a very pro-British Swiss enthusiast.

R. Gibson was riding a Velo in the 350 race and I myself was on a 500 Norton in the 500 c.c. class. Gibson retired in the early stages with engine trouble, and that left your humble the last hope.

We spent the interval carefully going over the Norton. The 500 class included Gileras, Guzzis, B.M.W.'s, Nortons, etc.

I had a good start and was lying fifth up to the half-way, quite happy, until I began to feel warm about the knees. Looking down, I saw petrol pouring from the carburetter!

I called in at the pits, but couldn't effect the necessary repairs, and to make it worse I couldn't refuel, for as the distance was only 100 miles one tank should have been sufficient and I had no further supply in the pit.

I set off again, not very happy, and as the race progressed I could still see the petrol running away and I guessed the winner must be almost near the end. I stopped and looked in the tank again—it was almost dry. I had a mile and a half to go and the crowd told me that Pagni, the winner, was on his last lap. I set off again, praying that I should have enough petrol. I had, but I received the chequered flag on a dead engine! We were both given our watches, and I had a nice silver trophy for sixth place.

THAT MOUNTAIN MIST

By Manliff Barrington.

I shall never forget what happened to me during my first appearance in the I.O.M., in 1934, when I was entered for the Lightweight T.T.

I was feeling very confident, for during the last morning's practice I had completed two laps in quite reasonable times in spite of considerable mist on the Mountain. However, feeling I could possibly do a bit better I started with good intentions on my third lap, but as I was approaching the fast left-hand bend near the Shepherd's Hut the mist suddenly became so thick that visibility was reduced to a couple of yards or so. Before I had time to realise my predicament I had lost my bearings. Without delay I applied the brakes and hoped for the best—but alas, it was too late, for I had overshot the bend and was heading straight for a drain on the outside of the corner. Within a couple of seconds I had been cast off the machine and was lying, completely winded and rather shaken, in the middle of the road.

After what seemed like many minutes a shepherd arrived on the scene and started to pull me to the side of the road, but in the middle of this operation we heard the roar of a rapidly approaching engine. I was unable to move because in the crash I had badly damaged both my ankles. The shepherd, however, thought discretion was the better part of valour, and, leaving me where I was, he ran for safety. The noise of the machine now seemed very close and the next second I was horrified to hear the screech of skidding tyres, and out of the mist I saw a machine coming straight towards me. I closed my eyes and expected the worst, but luck must have been on my side, for the machine swerved and in the process crashed headlong into my own badly bent racer. There was a moment of absolute silence and then I heard a string of the most fearful oaths from the apparently uninjured rider, demanding (more or less) what the so and so I and my machine were doing there.

When I explained matters the rider kindly offered to take me back to the start on his pillion. By this time I discovered I could manage to walk with great difficulty and when we had disentangled the machines we started off. I was still feeling a bit shaken, and I shall never forget the trip back, for the annoyed rider gave the machine the works all the way. More than once I felt like passing out, and only with difficulty managed to hang on. However, all's well that ends well, and it was not long before we arrived in one piece at the pits.

I then had the sad experience of having my brand new riding boots cut open to get them off my very swollen ankles.

This incident regrettably put paid to my racing in the Island in 1934.

THEY'D ALL GONE HOME
By Alec Bennett.

The 1923 Senior T.T. was a Very Wet Ride. It rained hard from start to finish, and I seemed to have one trouble after another, including the losing of a front mudguard, which did not help matters.

I eventually finished ninth, in time for a replica, but on crossing the finishing line I was surprised to find nobody about to flag me in. Not a soul to be seen, not even a pit attendant.

I proceeded to the marquee, where usually one finds a full house after the Senior, and there again the place was empty —even the bar attendant was missing. I began to think I was dreaming, but anyway I knew I was thirsty, so I set about climbing over the bar in search of something good to drink. Just as I got on top of the counter, the attendant popped out from behind some cases and said " Caught you! Who are you, and what do you want?" Not realising that my face was covered with mud and grit, I was a bit surprised at this, as he knew me quite well. However, I eventually received the very much needed whisky, and as I was soaked to the skin and very cold I naturally drank quite a lot of the good stuff.

On making enquiries as to where all the people were, I was told they had all gone home long before the race finished, owing to the heavy rain and cold wind. I have ridden in a good many road races, but never have I experienced such hardship as in that 1923 Senior and never did I want a drink more!

SERAFINI—MOLTO PRESTO

By Fred Frith.

Of all the many incidents which happen to a road racer perhaps the most vivid, certainly the most shattering in my own recollection, is one that occurred during the 1939 Ulster Grand Prix.

About halfway through the race I had a very slender lead in the 500 class over Serafini on the blown four Gilera. We were both circulating round the Clady course at an average of about 96-97 m.p.h., which wasn't exactly slow.

I remember soon after we had started the seventh lap we were flying along the four-mile straight from Ballyhill to Thorn Cottage. I had my chin jammed well into the tank-top pad, feet on the rearward footrests, elbows in, and was doing everything I knew to urge the bicycle along. I suppose the speed was around 118-120—that was about the Norton's maximum in those days.

Of course, I wasn't surprised to see Serafini draw alongside, but I was rather staggered to see him sitting almost upright and taking his ease. What really shook me, and at the same time gave me a feeling of complete and utter helplessness, was to see Serafini give me a friendly grin, take a large handful of grip, and disappear into the blue. Phew!!!!

For a moment or two I almost felt like stopping. That quickly passed, however, and soon I was trying as hard as before. But I never caught sight of the brilliant Italian combination again until the race was over.

CONTINENTAL CONTRETEMPS

By Jim Whalley.

The most thrilling ride I remember was in the 1921 Junior (my first T.T.) when I rode the Massey-Arran. Five miles from the finish, when I was leading, the tyre started to go down, and I took a crash. After gathering up all the bits and pieces, including a very long exhaust pipe—red hot!—I somehow managed to ride a much-damaged machine, with the bits and pieces draped all round me, into fifth position.

A very different sort of " thrill " happened one time when I went over for the Belgian Grand Prix. When I arrived at Antwerp somehow it happened that I was mistaken for a film star. Crowds of people, including reporters, photographers and mademoiselles were pulling me around and asking if I minded being called Douglas? Considering I was going to ride a Douglas motor cycle, I, of course, agreed. Imagine my surprise—and theirs!—when I realized I had been taken for Douglas Fairbanks! I'm afraid the interest waned rapidly when I was found to be after all only a racing motor cyclist.

Another anxious moment was when I was coming down the mountains in Spain (where I won the King of Spain's Gold Cup) and a wild pig, followed closely by a large litter, suddenly crossed the road in front of me.

Yet another thrill happened at San Sebastian (Spain), when I turned somersault, doing about 70 m.p.h., and broke a leg —yet I carried on and finished third. I had 120 miles to ride —including a fill-up—after the spill. It was certainly a hell of a business, though I did not know until I had finished that my leg was actually broken. This was due to the fact that I had on strong boots plus very heavy and tightly laced leather leggings, which held my leg together as tight as a splint would have done. When I took them off my leg was soon almost twice its normal size. The doctor went mad, and injected me to prevent tetanus. Luckily it was only a simple fracture, and I was able to walk with a stick in about seven weeks. After the spill naturally I only had the use of one leg, but I was determined to finish. There was a large money prize for the fastest lap—which I had already made—but to get the prize the rider had to finish the course; so I did.

DODGING THE DIVOTS

By Austin Munks.

One morning during practising for the 1934 M.G.P., when the sun was really shining and conditions were ideal, Crasher White on a Junior Norton and myself on a Junior Velocette came across each other and decided to have a first-class Grand Prix of our own.

This went on for a lap and a half, with first one and then the other in the lead. All went well until we arrived at the Nook for the second time with Crasher some fifty yards ahead. He rushed round the Nook—which as you know only too well is blind owing to the banks—I in turn dashed round after him, and to my surprise and horror I saw Crasher yards up the bank on the far side of the road, tearing chunks of grass and earth up with his footrests, etc. I couldn't do anything about it, having got the model well laid over, and I suddenly realised that Crasher and the model looked like falling on top of me. By sheer luck I just got under him before he stalled and decided to come to earth again. I actually rode through showers of earth and grass from the elevated Crasher, and dashed off to the finish, not being able to do anything about it myself.

When I was cutting the motor to come into the enclosure, to my amazement there was another machine just coming alongside, and of all people who should it be but one J. H. White—having come down from the bank still on board, taking no notice of what might have been swept away, and apparently only having one thought in mind: to be home with that Velocette!

STRONG MAN STUFF

By Harry Langman.

The day before the 1923 Sidecar T.T. race, I persuaded my passenger, Mainwaring, to fit a small screen to the sidecar body, to ward off the flying stones up the Mountain. He had complained of these during the practices, but didn't like the idea of anything obstructing his view. So finally the screen was put on and fastened securely with bolts, nuts and large washers through the body; but it wasn't tried out. Mainwaring, by the way, came from a family of weight-lifters, and was very strong. As we started off, on Race day, and got into the out-of-control feeling down Bray Hill, there was a sudden wrenching and splintering. I gave a quick glance to my left, and saw that the windscreen had gone, together with a large portion of the body. Mainwaring had pulled the lot off, and thrown it away—just like that!

NOT QUITE T.T.
By Jock West.

I doubt whether the I.O.M. Police have ever charged a competitor with being " under the influence " while competing in the T.T., but in 1935 I came very close to achieving this doubtful distinction!

This is how it happened. The day before the Junior, in which I was due to ride an N.S.U., I felt like death warmed up, due to a sudden attack of 'flu. Thanks to large and regular doses of whisky and lemon, plus a considerable number of aspirins, I felt much better on the Monday morning, but still very shaky. It was therefore arranged that if I got as far as the petrol stop there would be a " short " waiting for me. The motor ran beautifully, it was a glorious day, and in due course I pulled into the pits for machine and personal re-fuelling. Everything functioned as arranged and while attending to the quick filler with my left hand I found no difficulty in disposing of the contents of the glass that had been thrust into my right.

As I knocked the liquid back I thought that it seemed un-usually potent and by the time I arrived at the top of Bray Hill a very definite internal glow was becoming apparent, and it dawned on me that my request for a " short " had received such conscientious attention that I had been given a treble brandy!

By Quarter Bridge I was feeling fine and by Braddan I had a job deciding which road to take. From Union Mills to Ballacraine the road seemed extremely narrow and I remember hoping against hope that the motor would keep going, as I was certain that I was for Gaol House if for any reason at all I stopped. It has been said that drivers " under the influence " only imagine that they are driving well and that in fact they are hopelessly inefficient. On this occasion I proved to my satisfaction that I was taking some bends " flat out " that in the past had been treated with considerable respect and a noticeable drop in engine revs.

Luckily the effect of the alcohol lasted only a short time, owing to my exertions, and in due course I pulled into the pits for my second fill. Imagine my surprise when another glass of amber liquid was produced! There was no time to argue or explain and my attendant, realising that the refreshment was not needed, placed the glass on the coping in front of the pit. As soon as I had taken on sufficient fuel I threw the still gushing quick-filler into the depôt and passed on.

Having completed his duties for the day and feeling that he deserved some reward for his labours, my attendant made short work of the drink I had refused. Unfortunately for him, in throwing away the fuel filler a considerable quantity of petrol benzole had diluted the brandy, and for days he dare not risk a cigarette!

NOT QUITE T.T.

By Geoff Davison.

When I was in the early forties, I became ill, as is so often the case with men in the early forties. So I went to my doctor, who, besides being my doctor, was an old school-friend with whom I had knocked back many a half-pint in the good old days.

" The trouble with you, Geoff," he said, " is too much beer and not enough exercise. You don't want to be like an old man of fifty, do you—drinking beer and taking no exercise?"

It sounded like heaven to me, but I said: No I didn't. So I cut down the beer, and took some exercise. I even bought a bicycle.

When I was in the early fifties, I became ill, as is so often the case with men in the early fifties. So I went to my doctor, who, besides being my doctor, was—well, the same doctor as in paragraph one.

" The trouble with you, Geoff," he said, " is too much beer and not enough exercise. You don't want to be like an old man of sixty, do you—drinking beer and taking no exercise?"

It sounded better than ever to me, but I said: No, I supposed I didn't. And I fitted new tyres to the bicycle.

When I am in the early sixties, I shall become ill, as is so often the case with men in the early sixties. And I shall go to my doctor, provided that he hasn't died of the drink, and he'll say: " The trouble with you, Geoff . . . . "

And I shall say: " No ruddy fear—I've heard that story before." *And I shall sell him the bicycle!*

TWENTY YEARS OF RACING
By HAROLD DANIELL.

[*In 1946 Harold Daniell gave a very interesting talk on his motor cycling experiences to the Ravensbury M.C.C. His notes for that talk, brought up to date by references to 1947 and 1948, form the basis of this article*]

I started motor cycling in 1925, but it was not until 1929 that I took up racing seriously. This year of 1948, therefore, is my twentieth at the racing game.

In 1925 my father bought an A.J.S. twin, complete with two-seater sidecar, and it was on this machine, at the age of fifteen, that I took to the road after a few lessons from the local agent who supplied the outfit. In those days a licence to drive a motorcycle could be obtained by anyone over fourteen years old, and there were no L plates or driving tests, but against this we had a 20 miles per hour speed limit on all roads. This I soon found out—at my father's expense. I was pinched at such regular intervals that it must have cost about a pound a time to open the garage doors! I suppose the sight of a schoolboy flying along on a big-twin outfit was enough to make any policeman's mouth water.

At the end of 1926 my father bought me my first machine, a second-hand 1925 Model 18 Norton, and I rode this machine daily to Chelsea, where I had started on a two-year course in motor engineering. This bike was a '' bit of a monster '' to me at first, and I confess that it was not long before I applied to the A.A. for a route to Chelsea which would avoid tramlines!

Motor cycling had now '' got me '' and at every opportunity I was in the saddle. One Sunday afternoon in March, 1927, I was out joy-riding between Farningham and Sevenoaks when I spotted a group of motorcyclists in a nearby field. I stopped to investigate, and found that a hill climb was about to start and that these fellows were members of a motor cycle club, the Sydenham and District M.C.C. Entries were being taken on the spot and non-club members were allowed to compete. That was good enough. I entered my first event, and by a stroke of luck—it must have been luck —I won my class and a gold medal.

I became a member of the club and confidently entered for the Farningham hill-climb. It was a well supported event and many famous riders of the time were competing. My bike had been stripped of all unnecessary gear and towed some fifteen miles to the meeting. I only made one run, during which my clutch started slipping. I was promptly eliminated, but it was valuable experience, and I was able to study for the first time some of the pukka race bikes which were there—some drilled like sieves, with sprint petrol tanks, racing carburetters, and no oil tanks, the engine being primed with sufficient oil before the start of the run. All this was new to me, and in any case quite beyond my pocket at the time.

In 1928, the Crystal Palace Motor Cycle Racing Club was formed, and started their series of path races in the grounds of the Crystal Palace. After seeing the first meeting I decided to join the club, and at the second meeting I was one of the competitors. The riders were divided into two groups, Grade A, and Grade B, decided, I believe, on practice times. Much to my disgust I found myself grade A. Another lesson had been learned—never to show your true performance when practising.

I was out of the picture for the first few meetings, for, if I didn't fall off, something would fall off the bike. It was amazing how many little things could go wrong, but I was learning, the hard way, that preparation of a machine does not finish at the engine—the cycle parts are just as important. At the end of the season I was getting my fair share of wins, and if I could beat the others in the scramble for the first corner my chances were quite rosy.

I had now started work, and by June, 1929, had saved sufficient to purchase my first new bike. This was another Model 18 Norton and the season at the Palace was a very successful one for me, including, as it did, the Crystal Palace Solo championship with lap record. That year I took my holiday in June and went to see the T.T. for the first time. I thoroughly enjoyed the races and never missed a morning practice, as a spectator. I was disappointed that I was not eligible for the Amateur T.T. races, being employed in the Motor Trade, but the following year the " Amateur " was replaced by the Manx Grand Prix, and this rule no longer applied.

The 1930 season consisted of grass-track racing, and my savings, assisted by cash awards from my successes, enabled me to purchase a new and suitable machine for the I.O.M.

and to enter for the Senior M.G.P. I bought a C.S.1 Norton with special this, that and the other—the International Model did not come out until 1932. Dope fuel was permitted and I made arrangements with the Hammersmith Distillery Co. for 50 galls of PMS2 to be sent over.

By present day standards the machine was a touring affair, 3.25 x 19 in. tyres, front and rear, and three speed gearbox. It had a tiny leather pad on the rear mudguard, just for padding and definitely not for sitting on, as is the present practice. I well remember my first day's practising, and getting the impression that surely the motor must blow up with all this flat out blinding! My first lap was at exactly 60 miles per hour, with which I was quite satisfied. This made me over confident, for in the next morning's practice I hit the sandbags at Creg-na-Baa, well and truly. Fortunately no damage was done either to myself or to the machine, and I think, now, that it was a good thing I did pile up early on, for it taught me to respect the T.T. course.

The engine gave no trouble during the practices, and as it was my first O.H.C. motor I shirked taking it down until the Saturday. I had improved my lap speed to 64 m.p.h. but even so I was not too satisfied with the speed of the bike. On removing the cylinder head and barrel I found a beautiful flat top petrol-benzole piston. No wonder the motor ran cool and gave no trouble! Fortunately Nortons had a Depôt in Douglas for servicing the M.G.P. bikes, and the correct piston was obtained. The last practice on the Monday saw a jump in my lap speed to 68.1, the fastest of the practices. I looked forward to being near the front in the race but on the first lap the bike spluttered to a standstill at the Bungalow—out of fuel. It did not take long to find out why: the tank had a split along the bottom weld.

In 1931 I entered for the Senior M.G.P again, and sent my C.S.1 back to the works to be modernised. It came back with a new frame, four speed gearbox, inclined and offset inlet port, three inch front tyre, etc., and was generally similar to the International model which was introduced at the Show that year. Again large quantities of dope were sent to the Island, and I started practice with a useful 69.6 m.p.h. lap. The second practice morning, on my second lap approaching Signpost corner, there was a horrible crunch underneath me, followed by an even more horrible quietness. One glance at the motor was enough, a big hole had appeared in the front of the crankcase, and the front down tube had been flattened—even the magneto was knocked off!

Then followed two days hard labour. My brother and I worked into the night rebuilding the model, which was out again for the Friday morning's practice with a gentle lap at 56 m.p.h. On the last morning I recorded 72.2 m.p.h., the fastest senior lap of practice and 27 seconds inside the lap record. I was full of confidence, of course, on race day, but after covering only five miles on the first lap, the bike began to snake. Damn it, I thought, a puncture. It did not take long to trace the cause of the trouble. It was not a puncture —the rear wheel spindle had broken. Again I was to be a spectator.

I used that Norton on the grass during 1932, and it was this year that Syston Park racing was re-opened by the Grantham & District M.C.C. I entered for two Meetings, one in May and the other in August. The attraction to me to go so far, was " The Manx Race," with a prize of £20 towards entry and expenses for the coming Grand Prix. I had a field day, winning the Manx Race, the 500 c.c. race and also the solo race for the first eighteen from the first two events.

Donington Park was now becoming popular, and they were holding a two-day meeting at August Bank Holiday weekend. On the second day's racing they too were offering £20 towards entry and expenses for the M.G.P. If I could win this race, it meant that I could afford to ride in the Junior

M.G.P. as well as the Senior. So my programme was—
Syston on Monday, Donington on Tuesday.

What a week-end that was! The old Norton and sidecar
float which I was using at the time was weighed down with
tins of dope and oil, spare plugs, sprockets and chains, and
tools and leathers and crash hats. I collected the 500 c.c.
race at Syston, and was second in the 1100 c.c. event. The
float was loaded up again, and off we went to Donington,
where I had fixed up for the night at the famous Hall. We
had to get up early to practise, select a suitable sprocket and
generally prepare the machine. The results were 1st in the
Manx Race, 2nd in the 500 c.c. and 1st in the Unlimited.
We plodded home the same evening, tired but very satisfied
with the week-end's work.

I now had two Manx entries but only one bike, so I put
round feelers to the manufacturers for a good second-hand
Junior mount, eventually purchasing a J.A.P. engined Excelsior, which had been a spare practice job in the previous
June races. Dope was barred that year, a decision which
pleased everyone; it had been an expensive nuisance before,
because the slight advantage to be gained by its use could not
be ignored.

Practising was completed without serious trouble. The
Junior mount was a little down on maximum, and some valve
spring breakages and " mixing of valves " had occurred.
New valves and springs were fitted for the race, and I started
with visions of a replica rather than a win. The bike ran
well for the first five laps, and I was just off the leader board.
On the last lap she began to misfire at speed, and I knew
that the springs were failing. Added to this the offside footrest swung down, and had to be lifted out of the way on
right hand corners. I felt greatly relieved when I passed
Keppel Gate on the last lap, knowing that at least I would
finish even if I coasted from there to Governer's Bridge and
pushed in the last few hundred yards. The motor kept going,

however, and I collected my first silver replica, finishing ninth.

The weather had not been too kind for the Junior—the roads had been wet in parts and there had been some mist on the mountain—but the Senior race day was a record for sheer filthiness—pouring rain all the time and thick mist. Even at the start two of the riders skidded when mounting their bikes. I set off, already wet through, and groped my way round at 63.96 m.p.h. On the first lap I was in fifth place, 4 m.p.h. down on the leader. I cautiously increased my speed on each remaining lap and finished second at 66.97 m.p.h. to Norman Gledhill, who won at 67.32 m.p.h. I shall never forget that ride; wet, cold, flares on the mountain road to guide the competitors. How the bike kept going through all the water I don't know. It had no special preparation against weather, but it ran perfectly throughout, and was quite fast enough for the owner under such conditions! Many retired with waterlogged mags. and oiled-up plugs, due to cruising through the mountain mist. I had been very lucky in this respect, and was quite pleased with the results obtained.

In October I entered my first event at Brooklands. I had never seen the place before, but knew that outer circuit handicaps were not my " cup of tea." What interested me was the Senior Mountain Championship, on the well-known mountain circuit. The bike was used as in the Manx, except that I raised the compression to suit " dope " and fitted the regulation silencer. C. J. Williams on a (J. S. Worter's) Douglas and Ernie Nott on a Rudge led the race with myself within striking range. At half distance, Nott disappeared with engine trouble, and later cn the Douglas began to slow down, owing to the front brake lever coming up against the handlebars. This enabled me to slip by, two laps before the finish, and to win by five yards.

I had a busy season in 1933, as I competed at all the Donington Bank Holiday Meetings, and also at Brands

Hatch and Layhams Farm and Brooklands, all on the same machine, the 500 Norton. My second appearance at Brooklands was in the Clubman's Day Meeting. I had entered two five-lap Mountain Handicap Races, but my previous performance had not been forgotten, and I found myself scratch. I was unplaced in the first race and second in the other. I also entered the Brooklands 100 miles Grand Prix in August, but retired on the 11th lap with a flat tyre. Why the tyre went down I never found out, for the tube appeared perfect when tested.

For the 1933 M.G.P. the 500 was re-conditioned and modernized, including the fitting of a bronze cylinder head. I also purchased a new 350 Norton for the Junior event. The practising was completed without incident. In the Junior Race, I retired on the fourth lap with a seized engine, and at the time I was lying third.

In contrast to 1932, the weather for the Senior was perfect, a bright sunny morning and a very nice change from the showery and misty weather of which the September races had had more than a fair share. I shall not forget my first lap. The bike seemed so slow that I was sure something was wrong, but everything seemed to be working all right, just an apparent loss of perhaps 5 m.p.h. My pit signal at the end of the first lap was " O.K."—actually I was in the lead, but of course in the first lap with only one signalling point the only information I could expect was " O.K. " or " N.B.G." at the discretion of my pit attendant! On my second time round, my signal was 1+7 and I could not believe it—leading the race by seven seconds. The bike was slow, and yet leading!

Actually the bike was going perfectly, and I have noticed the effect many times since. It is due, I think, to the greatly improved visibility at mid-day as compared with early morning practice, and it is the more marked on those rare occasions when the race is run in perfect weather. At the start of the last lap my signal was 1+2½m. I was now in a position to take it easy and I was just easing up a little when No. 32, J. Swanston came alongside me. My number was 37, and as we started at half-minute intervals, he was obviously the second man and my nearest rival. Foolishly, I suppose, we raced to the finish, crossing the line within a few yards of each other. This is the only time I have actually raced against my nearest rival in the I.o.M. My average speed was 76.98 and Swanston collected the lap record on the last lap, at 77.86. At last I had won a " Manx."

I now turned to the June T.T. races and fixed up to ride for A.J.S., as required by them, during 1934, '35 and '36. I secured three T.T. replicas and won the 1936 Leinster 200, 350 c.c. class. At the same time I used my Manx Nortons at Donington and Brooklands with considerable success, including winning all three solo races at the Easter Monday Meetings and the 350 c.c. Mountain Championship at Brooklands.

It was during this year—1934—that I met Steve Lancefield, who was as keen on tuning and repairing racers as I was on riding, and he asked me to try out his own 500 Norton at Donington. It was the same specification as mine, but had been considerably lightened. The result was that the two 500 machines were taken to a Donington Meeting for comparison. Steve's bike proved to be better, and it was arranged that I would ride and he would prepare his own 500 bike. Apart from the 1934 Ulster Grand Prix for which I entered my Manx winner (the " steam roller," as Steve called it) I rode his 500 for several years, and my confidence in his tuning was fully rewarded. For example, in 1937 the 500 was unbeaten, winning every race entered, at Donington, the Brooklands Campbell circuit, and the Crystal Palace Road Course.

The " steam roller " was brought up to date for the 1934 Ulster at Nortons, and I received it just in time for the event. On testing the bike on the Clady straight, the speed was very disappointing, to put it mildly, and as we did not go prepared to do any tuning we spent many hours chasing all over Belfast for a timing disc, C.C. glass and other necessary tools we had left behind. I only managed to get in two practice laps, which was sufficient to qualify, and we went out again on the straight the afternoon before the event, for the final tune-up. The performance was now O.K.

While we were out testing we saw another competitor checking carburetter settings. He had an old and very standard International Norton, complete with rear wheel discs and bald tyres. The owner was gazing at his sparking plug, which appeared as if it had been in a furnace. The mixture was obviously much too weak, so we fixed him up with a jet which would at least keep the motor going without seizing. Well it did, because this machine beat me into second place for the handicap award!

Thanks to an excellent get-away, I missed the tremendous pile-up that occurred at Ballyhill, a fast sweeping right hand bend, half a mile from the start. Guthrie had come off and being a massed start with the 350 c.c. machines following a few seconds later there was a terrific scramble to dodge fallen riders and machines. Some fifteen competitors from both classes were out of the race almost as soon as it started. On my second lap I could not fail to notice the great number of bikes lying alongside the road and guessed that something serious had happened. The model ran well but I was forced to make an extra stop to refill with oil after losing the oil filter cap towards the end of the race. I finished fifth at 84 m.p.h. and second on handicap as I have already mentioned.

This has been my only finish in the Ulster—in fact the circuit has spelled bad luck for me ever since. The following year, 1935, riding an A.J.S., I was forced to crash to avoid a fallen rider at Aldergrove corner. When I came to, I was in a hut in the nearby aerodrome, but I was not alone for

Walter Rusk was on the next bed, also a victim on the
same corner, having been in a mix up with Guthrie, who was
able to continue and win.

I was taken to the hospital in Belfast, where they wanted
to keep me over night. I had other ideas, however, and did
not fancy staying behind until the next boat, which would
not be until Monday night. I could not escape, having in-
sufficient clothing, and I was just giving up hope when Jock
West appeared with my things, and in a flash I was out, just
catching the Saturday night boat!

For the 1936 Ulster Grand Prix Nortons offered me a run
in the 350 c.c. class, my first ride on a " really and truly "
works racer. My first impression of this machine reminds
me of the Persil advert.—" I thought my bikes were good
until I tried Joe Craig's!". After promising practice times I
started with every chance of winning, but this was the Ulster
Grand Prix. On the first lap, buzzing along the Clady
straight, the motor cut out. It cut in again at low speeds,
but would not open up. I quickly changed the plug, but the
result was the same, and I toured in to retire. The trouble
was that the nipple had come off the air wire at the carburetter end, so allowing the air slide to close. Even if I
had spotted the trouble straight away, it would have taken
too long to remove the slide completely and still be in the
running.

The 1937 season was easily the most successful one I had
on non-works mounts. At the Easter Monday Donington
meeting I was second in the 350 race and first in the 500.
Then came the opening meeting on the New Crystal Palace
Road Course. I was second in the Junior Coronation Grand
Prix, and won the Senior Coronation G.P. after an exciting
finish. My rear brake rod came adrift in the 25th lap, and
for the remaining five laps Stanley Woods and Jock West
began to overhaul me. One more lap and the result would
have been entirely different, and as it was 50 yards covered
the first three of us at the finish.

On the Whit Monday at Donington I was again second on the 350—Maurice Cann was the menace that year. I won the 500 c.c. Race and also the 50 mile Coronation Trophy Race. I had on order a new 350 Norton for the T.T., as my 1933 350 was now a trifle out of date. Steve had modernised the 500 year by year—it was a 1934 model originally. So we left for the Island with an unknown 350 and a quite well known 500.

The practising weather was generally pretty filthy, and apart from slight clutch trouble, which was soon rectified, the new bike showed promise. It ran perfectly throughout the race and I finished fifth at 78.77, the first private owner home. On the morning of the weigh-in for the Senior, the model was taken on the mountain road for a final check-up and carburetter setting, and on one of the flat out runs the engine seized! You can imagine our feelings with the bike due to be handed in in a few hours time. The engine was free by the time I had pulled up, and we had visions of a scored piston. It was too risky to start the motor up again for fear of causing further damage, so we towed her in and pounced on her, whipping off the head and barrel in record time. Everything was perfect! The trouble was traced to the engine shock absorber, the back face of which had picked up on to the adjacent crankcase face. The parts were cleaned up and the clearance increased—there was a small crack in the crankcase which had to be ignored. There was also a risk that the timing side bearing might have been shifted slightly, which would also affect the meshing of the bottom bevels, but time was too short for more than a rough check. The bike was handed in late, for which the A.C.U. relieved me of one pound!

Owing to the poor practice weather, we had never had an opportunity of really checking fuel consumption—we thought we could do the race with one fill-up, but we were not sure. We decided to see how the bike performed during the race and take a chance if necessary. As it happened, the bike went so well that at the end of the fifth lap I was lying fourth. I had to decide now, during the sixth lap whether to stop for fuel and possibly lose a place, or carry on with the risk of stopping completely. I tried to see if there was enough petrol in the tank by opening the filler cap towards the end of the circuit, but the splashing and surging of the fuel made it impossible to judge exactly how much there was. I decided to stop and fill up. This dropped me back to fifth position, as I had expected, and I completed the race at an average speed of 83.61, again being first private entry home.

In July, Nortons offered me a ride in the 500 class of the Dutch T.T. Owing to a misunderstanding as to the boat times, I arrived at Harwich to see the boat disappear. I stayed the night at Harwich and caught the boat next day. By making signs and showing my railway tickets, I arrived at Assen the following morning in the early hours. At one point in the journey I very nearly boarded a train for Essen, which would have been an entirely different story. Anyway, there I was at the right place, but Norton's depôt *would* have to be at the other side of the course. I eventually obtained a lift to the depôt just before the final practice started.

Joe Craig was none too pleased at my late arrival, and at first was not inclined to let me compete. I said I had not come all this ———— way just the watch the ———— race. Eventually I was allowed to practise, and had only time to do seven laps and qualify. I had been very impressed by the performance of the 350 works machine in the 1936 Ulster, but this 500 was terrific—and one of the fastest circuits in Europe, completely strange to me, is not the ideal place to get used to a machine of this performance. I could quite see now why Joe was not too keen for me to race with so little practice! However, everything turned out O.K. and I finished second to Karl Gall on the B.M.W. at the speed of 80.6 m.p.h.

My next event was the open meeting on the Campbell Road Circuit at Brooklands, when I won the Junior and Senior

Road Championship Races. On the August Monday Donington Meeting there were two 20 lap Solo Grand Prix Races, which I added to my collection.

Nortons again offered me a mount for the German Grand Prix, 350 class. There was no serious opposition to the Nortons in this class and it was agreed that Crasher White and I would keep together during the race and fight it out for first place on the last two laps. We raced neck and neck for those two final laps, approaching the last corner, a sharp left hand turn, some 50 yards from the finish, wheel to wheel. You can imagine the two of us, each waiting for the other to shut off for this last corner. I shut off first and Crasher, leaving it just too late, went wide, touching the protective straw bags. This allowed me to slip through on the inside and win by a few yards. The 500 c.c. class race followed, and the whole meeting was marred by the tragic death of Jim Guthrie. My last event that year was the Brooklands Grand Prix, held on the Campbell Circuit, resulting in a win in both classes. I had been entered in the 500 c.c. class Ulster G.P. by Nortons, but as a mark of respect for Guthrie their entries were withdrawn.

At the end of the year I signed up as a member of the official Norton team for the 1938 season. My agreement excluded me from riding other than works machines and entries, so for that season Donington and Brooklands, etc., were out. The Nortons were considerably re-designed and did not arrive in the Island until the third practice morning. Until then I was using the Donington 500 which we had lent to Norman Croft for the Senior Race. On the second practice morning, the weather was very bad, and actually it was foolish of me to attempt practising, but I was keen to get a bit in. Just after Ballacraine I got into a slide at about 90 m.p.h. and caught a stone wall with the left hand foot-rest. In a flash I was off and the bike finished up on the opposite side of the road completely re-designed! I was pretty badly knocked about and after treatment at Nobles Hospital spent the rest of the day in bed, wondering how long it would be before I could be out again. Fortunately I was fit enough for Tuesday evening practice, and by race day was as good as new.

In the Junior Race my motor seized on the first lap, but kept going for the remainder of the race. I finished fifth, for the third time in succession, at 80.64 m.p.h. On the opening lap of the Senior Race I did not flatten the motor out until it was thoroughly warmed up, I was afraid of a repetition of Monday's seizure, and as a result my position was fourth at the end of the circuit. By now I was getting used to the monster, but I received no signals at Ramsey and only got a request for more speed each time I passed the pits. At the end of the third lap I stopped for fuel and oil and learnt that I was in third position, and was not going fast enough!

I was now riding all out and the only way to improve my speed was to thrash the motor. I had been driving on the rev. counter, and knowing that these instruments are far from reliable, I decided to drive by " feel." This proved success-ful and at lap six my signal at Ramsey was a large W with — 5 underneath. I was pleased to receive a signal at Ramsey at last—apparently I was in the race after all! But the W meant that Woods was leading, and that was not going to be a very popular result with the Bracebridge Street firm. I wondered where Freddie was lying—actually we were dead heated in second place. On my last lap past the pits my signal was " 2nd—3 " with frantic waving to supplement the sign. Actually I had a lead of 5 seconds at this point but as Woods' number was 30 and mine 15 the signal referred to my position at Ramsey.

On the last lap Ramsey Signal was " 1—5 " and I nearly fell off with excitement. I calculated that now I was in the lead I had only to maintain my speed and concentrate on avoiding mistakes—and then it would be in the bag! Actually, the final lap proved to be my fastest, and is the present lap

record of 24 m. 52.6 seconds—91 m.p.h. Woods was still
on the mountain when I finished and they were anxious
moments waiting for him to come in. Looking back at the
results, it is clear that the turning point of the race was in
the fourth lap, which included the time taken at the pit stop
for fuel and oil. This shows how important team work is
while replenishing. Here are the times of the first three men
for that lap—Frith, 26m. 16 secs.; Woods, 26m. 18 secs.; and
myself, 25 m. 54 secs. I had gained 24 secs. on Woods and
22 secs. on Frith on this one lap, and the race was won by 15
secs.!

The Belgian Grand Prix which followed proved a tough
nut. The course I found to be extremely difficult to learn,
with its hairpin and many bends-that-keep-on bending. The
sides of the roads fall away to a loose dusty surface, and I
think this was probably the biggest snag. The apparent width
was not the actual width of the road, and I had no desire to
broadside at road-racing speeds. Added to this the course is
dotted with monuments to racing drivers who have been vic-
tims on the circuit. The hot sun had melted the tar and vast
quantities of loose gravel were put down by the authorities;
these proved as bad as the tar from the point of view of road
adhesion.

The race started with a scrap between Jock West, Woods,
Frith and myself, with Meier leading. After about eight laps
Woods, taking to the loose stuff to pass a 250 c.c. competitor,
came unstuck, badly damaging his left hand. Frith had
pulled away slightly and was lying second to Meier, while
West and I were having a ding-dong battle for third place.
I managed to slip past Jock several times coming out of slow
corners, but the B.M.W. would leap ahead on the straights.
I was slip-streaming him at every opportunity but the
showers of gravel did not improve the motor, which slowed
towards the end of the race. I finished fourth at 89.13 m.p.h.
behind West, Frith and Meier, who won at 90.33. The front
of my machine after the race was amazing. All the enamel

had been sandblasted from the forks and the hub of the front
wheel.

The Swiss Grand Prix was held in Geneva over a short circuit of two miles, 60 laps to each race. The course included
tram-lines and a road divided by sand bags. The 350 race
was a battle between Frith and me until at about the 14th lap
when I drew ahead. My winning speed was 64.35 m.p.h.,
which gives some indication of the circuit.

In the 500 c.c. race, two blown Gileras, ridden by Aldrighettie and Serafini, jumped into the lead, but on the eighth
lap, Aldrighettie retired with a flat back tyre, and I got into
the lead which I retained to the finish, with Frith second.
During this race the brakes were becoming so hot that I found
I could actually stand on the brake pedal without any danger
of locking the wheel! The German Grand Prix followed, but
it was impossible to catch Meier on the B.M.W. and I had to
be content with second place.

The Ulster Grand Prix started with the road nice and wet
and Frith went off like a scalded cat with an opening lap of
93.77, with myself in second place at a mere 90.89. It was
a terrific lead after one lap and his speed proved to be his
undoing on the second circuit, when he slid down at Green-
mount, damaging the model. This left me in the lead with
Jock West second. The roads were drying and speeds went
up to 97 m.p.h., but with only two laps to go the bike slowed
on the Clady Straight. My rear wheel bearing had
failed, and I toured into the pits to retire as Jock West flashed
past. It is amazing that the bearings which had given no
trouble all through the season should not stand up to the
Ulster.

The official Nortons appeared at Donington for the first
time at the end of August in the Dunlop Jubilee Meeting.
After winning a very close race with Crasher White in the
350 c.c. class I took out the 500 c.c. dope " monster " for the
lap record attempt. After riding the 350 this machine seemed
to fly along, and although the record was raised to 77.48, I

am sure it could have been better, had I taken it out after riding a 500. In the 500 c.c. race Freddie Frith beat me into second place.

The last pre-war season—1939. Nortons had decided not to race officially and plans were made for entering the M.G.P. machines. Later, however, they offered the 1938 machines to Fred and myself. In the Junior T.T. the first lap positions were Frith, Fleischman, myself and Woods. On the second lap it started raining on the Ramsey side of the circuit and I slid to earth in Parliament Square, but got going again quickly as the motor did not stall. The rev. counter drive was broken off, and I stuck the loose end in between the front engine plates. By the next time round the roads had practically dried. I improved my speed towards the end and finished only eight seconds behind Woods, the winner.

In the Senior Race we carried small auxiliary petrol tanks on top of the ordinary petrol tank, and by turning on a tap the contents drained into the main tank. This was a last minute scheme, as the previous year we finished with just the smell in the tank! I cracked off determined to start with a quick lap at the beginning for a change, but just before Kirkmichael the motor seized. It freed and I continued, with considerably reduced revs. until, as a result of too much third gear work, I ran out of fuel at the Gooseneck on the fourth lap. On August Bank Holiday Monday I rode the works' bikes at Donington, winning all three races, and at the Grand Prix Meeting later in the month I finished second to Frith in the 350 and retired in the 500. That was my last pre-war race.

The rest of it is too recent to call for detailed narrative. I did not ride in the Island again for eight long years, but I came back to it in 1947 as keen and enthusiastic as ever. And once again my policy of " go slow to start with " paid me. I cracked off hard at the beginning of the Junior, was second on the first lap, third on the next and back to second again on the third, only to retire with engine trouble in the fourth.

In the Senior I had better luck, and my positions for each of the laps were second, first, second, first, first, second and first. After all, it's the last one that matters! The consistency of my lap times is interesting. Except for the fourth lap, which included the main fill-up, there were only 14 seconds between the slowest and the fastest—27 mins. 21 secs. the slowest and 27 mins. 7 secs. the best. Incidentally, my last lap, which included a " short " fill-up, was done in 27 mins. 14 1/5th secs. so, if it hadn't been for the stop, it would have been the quickest—as usual!

Things did not go so well in 1948. I ran third in the Junior for the first three laps, but on the fourth lap the oil tank split, and that was that. In the Senior, I had bad luck, too. Here again I was lying third—for the first four laps. On the fifth and sixth lap I was second, with Artie Bell leading me by 41 seconds. And then, on the last lap, near Kirkmichael, with just over twenty miles to go, my front chain broke.

Well, I'll be back again next year for my " 21st " . . .

MY FIRST T.T.
By Jack Marshall.

[*This article was first published in the T.T. Special in 1934, as were the three others which follow*]

I can certainly claim to be one of the veteran riders for my first T.T. was the first race ever held—in 1907. I rode a single-cylinder, single-geared Triumph, my stable companion being Frank Hulbert.

There seems to be some misapprehension as to what the T.T. was in those days. The official programme gives results of two races, the single-cylinder and twin-cylinder race, but the John Bull booklet describes these races as the Senior and the Junior respectively. Actually, of course, the former is correct, but there was only one trophy (which is the present Senior trophy) and this went to the fastest time of the day irrespective of class.

In 1907 we were limited, not by capacity, but by petrol consumption, single-cylinders having to average rather more than twins. We used the short course starting at St. John's, turning left at Ballacraine and following the present course to Kirk Michael and thence back to Peel and St. John's. This course was just under 16 miles in length and we did ten laps of it.

Most of the machines were fitted with pedalling gear, but the Triumphs, which Hulbert and I rode, were not so equipped. Creg Willies Hill, which was narrow and winding in those days assumed tremendous proportions. To climb it I had to nurse my engine the whole way from Ballacraine; on reaching Glen Helen I would open up, scrape round Creg Willies corner and get as far as I could up the hill, running the last few yards.

We had a trouble in the first T.T. which is not experienced by riders to-day—DUST. They used to spray the roads with some form of acid from a watering cart and this certainly laid the dust for the time being, but it also splashed up on to one's clothes and rotted them away. After a bit the acid lost its effect and the clouds of dust from any machine were terrific. Overtaking was extremely difficult, not to say dangerous. One charged blindly into a cloud of dust and hoped that there would be a clear road ahead on the other side of it, and that the cause of the dust would not wobble or swerve as one went past.

In the race itself I was unlucky in my very first lap. I got round the Devil's Elbow on the Kirk Michael—Peel Road all right, but I took the bend following it too fast, crashed into a pile of stones on the side of the road and came a purler. I damaged my knee and bent the machine a bit, but not too badly to carry on.

Off I went again on the second lap. At Ballig Bridge my back tyre burst. I took out the tube, repaired it and carried on once more. From that point I had a no trouble run and finished second, nine and a half minutes behind Charlie Collier on his Matchless.

By the way, we had to have efficient silencers without cut-outs in those days, and as we were also limited as regards petrol consumption, as the roads were very bad and as most of us were single-geared, average speeds of nearly 40 miles per hour were not too bad.

After the race there was some discussion as to whether I should have been able to beat Charlie Collier if I had not fallen off and also had not been delayed by the puncture. Obviously, there were many points on each side, so to settle it a match was staged at Canning Town race track between Charlie and Harry Collier on their Matchless's and Frank Hulbert and myself on our Triumphs. It was a five mile race over a quarter-mile track—twenty laps in all.

So far as I remember, Harry Collier and Hulbert were neck and neck in the lead and I was running third with Charlie Collier close behind. Then Harry and Hulbert collided. Hulbert crashed, but Collier managed to keep on although, of course, he slowed down. I had my eyes so glued to the line of the track I was riding round that I never saw Hulbert crash. I knew, however, that I passed Harry Collier and was very pleased with myself when, suddenly, they stopped the race. Even then I did not know what had happened. I thought perhaps the race was ended and that I had miscounted my laps. But they stopped it because of poor Frank Hulbert's crash, which was pretty serious. So that little race proved nothing.

The next year, however, we of the Triumph stable got our our back, for I managed to win, and the late Admiral (then Captain) Sir R. K. Arbuthnot, on a Triumph, was third with Charlie Collier second on his Matchless.

It may amuse some present day riders to be told that during my winning ride I broke an exhaust valve and replaced it, yet the machine averaged over 40 miles per hour and over 117 miles per gallon.

I must conclude this little article with two personal items: the first, a tribute to the Collier brothers, who were the finest sportsmen of the time, and the second, a very hearty invitation to all motorcyclists to " come and see me sometime " at the Royal Oak Hotel, Whitley, on the main London-Coventry Road, where we can " talk T.T. " till closing time.

MY FIRST T.T.

BY GRAHAM WALKER.

A lot of things have happened since 1920, but first impressions are lasting, especially when they leave scars! My experiences in the Senior T.T. of that year are almost as clear in my mind as last year's. The reason is not far to seek. Ever since my schooldays I had looked upon the T.T. as my particular idea of heaven, little dreaming that after the War I should join Norton Motors Limited, and become a " racer. ' During 1919, thanks to a very reliable machine and a great deal of luck, I had some moderate successes in speed trials and hill climbs. I thus came to the notice of that hardy old warrior, D. R. O'Donovan, when the time arrived to choose the team for the first post-war T.T.

" Don " was rightly of a cautious disposition, so he took me over to the Island to see how I shaped. I can see him now, standing on the bank at the Gooseneck, giving me kindly criticism and encouragement each time I took the famous bend. I was almost paralysed with " stage fright," and when I realised that I should have to do at least one practice lap in 60 minutes to qualify I felt like packing my bag and rushing away before I made a fool of myself and let the firm down. I owe " Don " a debt I can never repay for his kindness to me at that time.

During practising I had my share of excitement, as I hit a sheep when coming down to the Bungalow at about 60. I was lucky to get off with a black eye and a dislike for mutton which has lasted ever since. On another occasion I had a burst rear tyre, when Vic. Horsman, Noel Brown and Charlie North were right on my tail. It has never been settled which was the most frightened of the four of us!

We had twelve days' practising then, and it was needed, as the course was far harder to learn then than it is nowadays. Few of the present riders or spectators can have any conception of the circuit as it was at this time. The surface was very loose and the roads were abominably bumpy. There was no tar, consequently dust and stones were a terrible bugbear. It is a solemn fact that grass and moss grew up the centre of the track over the mountain, and the recent road-widening schemes of the Manx authorities had not yet been hatched. Two enormous manhole covers projected at the bottom of Bray Hill. Ballig Bridge was terrifying. Sulby Bridge looked barely wide enough to take one motor cycle, and on Ramsey we had to wander round some side roads instead of going straight up May Hill. The mountain road was called so by the locals, but what we called it depended upon our Army training. Windy Corner was chronic and the 33rd was a nightmare. The worst of all, however, was Keppel Gate, which was then a very narrow affair by the cottage, below the present imposing gate. It was the most amazing optical illusion I have ever seen, and it seemed impossible for a pair of handlebars to pass through it.

The best way I can express the difference between the course in 1920 and in 1934 is to say that then we prayed for the bends to give us an excuse to ease muscles tensed on the battering straights, whereas now we pray for the beautiful straights so that we can have a nice " lie down " after frightening ourselves on the bends. Another mystery is that in 1920 I was almost frozen to the marrow (what is the marrow?) in the early mornings, whereas nowadays I never feel the cold. To avoid rude people writing to me, I will volunteer the suggestion that then I weighed 12 st. 7 lbs., whereas now I never look a scale in the face, but have been told by the chemist that I am 14 st. 10 lbs.!

The machine I rode was the pride of my existence, but the harsh light of experience reveals it in all its crudity: 57½" wheelbase, which required a hinge in the middle when corners loomed up. Conversely, it felt just as if it had got a hinge in the middle when on the bumpy Sulby Straight. Side valve engine with colossal flywheel and a top gear of 4 to 1. A cast-iron piston, providing enough vibration to work a road drill, two-lever carburetter, just in case there wasn't enough to do with hanging on. Forks with 2 ins. movement, mostly in the wrong direction. Tyres 26 x 2¼ ins., ridden bone hard and warranted to attract nails like a magnet. A saddle as hard as charity; no mudguard pad, and a tank so narrow that even with knee-grips one was knock-kneed.

In my innocence I used a pair of " hill climb " handlebars with the grips situated near the front spindle. Never shall I forget those bars—it was only an extraordinarily stout body belt which prevented my kidneys from bursting through my back! Speed trial influence caused me to fit a piston which gave far too high a compression ratio for the plugs of that era, and in a moment of aberration I solemnly fitted a large square toolbag and complete kit of tools on the extreme end of the carrier (mark that, ye riders of to-day, I said on the carrier!). The combination of long wheelbase and heavy weight at the extreme end gave exactly the same results as one's boyhood experiments with a stone swinging at the end of a string!

The pièce-de-résistance, however, was the lubrication system. This consisted of a hand pump which one was instructed to pull up and down every four miles. I am methodical by nature, but method went to the winds with that pump. It was a case of " pump when courage was sufficient to let go with one hand," and special spots were selected for the operation and carefully memorised.

The great day, June 17th, 1920, eventually dawned. Arrayed in a borrowed waistcoat (property of Soresby, ex-1914 T.T., now with Amal) and a scrounged crash hat (ex-O'Donovan) I lined up, like most of the others, scared stiff. There were 27 starters, and I was No. 59 (in those days numbers ran consecutively through the series). Armed to the teeth

with spare plugs, tools and spare inner-tube I set sail like a
Spanish galleon before a fair breeze. The roads at first were
greasy, then later dazzlingly white and dusty. I was to learn
in this, my first race, that tinted goggles would be more sen-
sible next time.

I wrestled and struggled round Ballacraine and over Ballig,
where I landed long before my heart; through the Glen and
Kirk Michael's impossibly narrow street; over Ballaugh I
volleyed and thundered, only to meet my Waterloo after a
catch-as-catch-can down the Sulby Straight. Due to immature
judgment I approached far too fast. My descent to earth was
hastened by the fact that someone had told me resin was good
for brake blocks. I had therefore rubbed some on the shoes
of the front stirrup brake and the heat was just beginning to
have the desired effect. The Vee block and dummy belt rim
rear brake must have decided to leave all the pulling up to
the front brake, as it certainly did nothing for the rest of the
day. I came a fearful purler, and was only saved by the fact
that I wore my two spare inner tubes rolled up as a belt. These
acted as castors in the small of my back as I skated up to the
Bridge, which I met head on. In a daze I can remember
picking up the machine when it arrived a second or two later.

It was a sorry sight. As I attempted to straighten it up,
I dimly saw an intelligent pair of legs holding the front wheel
square. (These were subsequently identified as belonging to
the inimitable Bertie Boynton, of happy memory). Eventually I limped off again, badly crippled. The handlebars had
become " T.T." on one side and " full touring " on the
other. The footrests were a sorry mess, and the rear brake
pedal, whilst admittedly it had been only an ornament, had
now become a menace, as it dug me in the ankle. The saddle
nose clip was broken and, greatest tragedy of all, the knob
on the oil pump handle was missing. This meant that " every
four miles or when courage allowed " I had to pull the pump
spindle up with a pair of pliers and push it down with my bare

hand. I became quite expert at sheathing the pliers in my belt.

Personal damage consisted of a badly lacerated left knee which was subsequently found to be cracked, and a torn left palm which was not improved by the pumping business. A valuable lesson was learnt, however, and that was that no medals are granted for falling off. (Incidentally, Soresby's waistcoat and O'Donovan's helmet were now definitely second-hand).

In an endeavour to make up time I forced the poor old engine to such an extent that seven plugs gave up the ghost before the run was over, and I added blisters to my fingers when changing them as a further souvenir of the race I had always dreamed about.

When I came to fill up at the end of the second lap, the Norton crowd tried to stop me going on, and I have vivid recollections of little Bill Hassall (another man to whom I owe a lot of thanks) hanging on to my leg until a backward kick from me hurled him into the pit. Bill was brought up in Birmingham, but he told me afterwards that my language was an education!

In the third lap my troubles were added to when the complete saddle top disappeared whilst going up the mountain. From there on I wished they had stopped me when I filled up, but no one was risking a kick when I filled up at the end of the 4th lap, and I was too dizzy to mention the saddle disaster. After that fill I changed more plugs in the fifth lap. Then with visions of finishing at last I girded up my loins and the remnant of my will power, but even then Fate was against me, and my last lap, like all the others, contained a stop. An apt summary of my day's experiences lay in my position—13th! My position for a week or two after that was in bed, either on my right side or on my front!

Nortons were very nice to me, however, as my finishing gave them 100 per cent. finishers in the official team, positions being Duggie Brown 2nd, Jimmy Shaw 7th, Noel Brown 8th,

Charlie North 10th, G.W.W. 13th. In addition Norman Slater was 4th, Norman Black 11th (incidentally on my old 1919 belt drive Philipson-Pulley machine which I sold to him just before the race), and Jack Thomas 14th, so altogether the Barons of Bracebridge-street showed promise of that wonderful reliability they have exhibited in recent years.

My souvenirs of the great day consist of several scars and a very nice cigarette case from Norton Motors Ltd. To these must be added a determination not to fall off if it can be avoided and a strong leaning towards comfort at all costs.

MY FIRST T.T.

BY THE LATE JIM GUTHRIE.

Nineteen twenty three saw me in the Island for the first time, very green to road racing. This was the first time I had ever tried it, having previously only done short distance sand racing and hill climbs.

To get a machine was quite an effort and then it was more or less a private entry. In the end a 350 Matchless was promised. This was also the first time Matchless had entered for a number of years.

F. W. Neill and Bert Colver (both from the Matchless factory) and the late Hugh Mason were the team. I was there —that was about all that could be said for me.

During practice my laps were as quick as any of the Matchless team (for which I was very thankful). I also had the honour of a morning out on the then new camshaft job for a try-out. It was, however, not quite ready, so Messrs. Collier decided not to use this machine for the race.

Fuel was our principal trouble—none of our team knew anything about the " stuff " so it was eventually decided to mix half and half R.D.1 and P.M.S.2 to get the good qualities of each. The results were not too good and all our machines packed up sooner or later.

I cannot remember how far I went in the race—but I know I didn't get another machine till 1927!

MY FIRST T.T.

By the late Wal Handley.

My first T.T. was the Lightweight race of 1922 which, incidentally, was the first real Lightweight held—previously there had been a Lightweight class which was run in conjunction with the Junior race.

For some years before then I had ridden in various reliability trials, speed trials and hill climbs on O.K. machines. I was employed at the time by O.K.'s and was very keen to try my luck in the T.T. Naturally, therefore, I welcomed Mr. Ernest Humphries' offer of a mount for the 1922 Lightweight race.

My first experience of the Island was, to say the least of it, unusual. In those days we had a full fortnight's practising. I arrived in Douglas on Tuesday evening of the first week and turned out to practise the following morning. I had never seen the T.T. course, and when I arrived at the playing fields on the Wednesday morning there was a heavy mist. I pushed on to the road with my machine half pointing to Governor's Bridge and was then told that I could go. I did—at full speed, the wrong way of the course!

There was a lot of excitement over that, as may well be imagined, and the marshals fairly danced about the road waving flags at me. I thought they had all gone mad, but by the time I reached Governor's Bridge I realised what was the matter and turned round.

The papers were very nasty about my lapse, which was not altogether my own fault—the officials might at least have shown a newcomer which way to go! One paper on the mainland came out with a headline " Comedy of the Novice from Birmingham,'' and there were a lot of caustic remarks underneath. I decided that I would have to show them something and on the Saturday of the first week's practising I succeeded in clipping about 3 minutes off the existing Lightweight record.

Machines, particularly lightweights, were not so fast in those days—the best my own would do was to lap Brooklands at 59. In the race itself I managed to put up a record lap from a standing start (which was allowed in those days) at 51, and if you consider all the corners and rough going of the 1922 course, you will realise that this did not give one much time to hang about on corners. On the first lap I led the ultimate winner by a few seconds, but packed up at Sulby on the second lap with engine trouble.

I never fell off at all that first year; I wish I could say as much for all the other years!

I still like the Lightweight race the best of the three. The slightly reduced speed of the machine gives one a fraction of a second more to weigh up a corner. I also liked the course as it was twelve years ago much better than that of to-day. Although the machines were so much slower, the roads were so narrow and winding that one was cornering all the time, so that more counted on the rider's capabilities than on the sheer speed of his mount.

WAL HANDLEY—AN APPRECIATION
By Geoff Davison.

[*By kind permission of "The Motor Cycle" in which paper this article was published on 25th December, 1941*]

MUCH has been written about Walter Handley and of what he did; but little has been said of his remarkable personality, or of how and why he was so outstanding in the world of speed.

I first met him twenty years ago, and for the last ten years I have counted him among my closest friends. As one grows older one loses many friends, but never have I felt so irreparable a loss as when I read that paragraph in the daily Press: " Walter L. (' Wally ') Handley, known to motor racing enthusiasts as ' the man who would not be frightened,' was killed in an aeroplane crash on Saturday . . . One of the most dare-devil track motorcyclists and car drivers, Handley had several times escaped death." I can picture the expression on his face if he could have read that paragraph; he would have said, I think, just—" Ah, you Press-men again!"

It was through Ernest Humphries that I first met him, in the spring of 1922. Ernest had entered Walter for the Light-weight T.T., and in introducing him said: " I've got a boy here who can ride rings round you." Walter, very shy (he would have been nineteen, I think), looked at the floor and said, " How do?" He must have known then that he was better than the best of us, but had not proved himself, and was diffident before Ernest's glowing praise.

The proof came in the Lightweight race. True to his later form—in fact, it was in that race that he established his form—he set off at a cracking speed and put in a record lap from a standing start. He broke down in the second lap and left me easy going. After the race I said to him, " Bad luck." He said, " Ah!"

I next met him in the French Grand Prix—or rather, saw him there, at the side of the road, broken down. He waved gaily, and it was the first time I saw him smile. Soon after came the 1922 Belgian Grand Prix, where again he was my main rival. Who of us who rode in it will ever forget that dreadful race, when the heavens opened and the accumulated rain of weeks fell on our ill-clad bodies and unprepared machines? About ten of us started in the " 250 " class, and by half-way there were two of us left—Walter and I. Soaked to the skin, numbed and stiff with cold, we staggered on. Both of us were in dire trouble: Walter with a water-logged mag-neto, I with bad overheating due to a mud-clogged cylinder. Each lap we passed and repassed each other, and each time, no matter which of us was on the move, he gave me a cheery wave and that gay laugh which, as I came to know later, was characteristic of him in adversity. He laughed often when racing, but the real gaiety came only when everything was going dead wrong. We came in first and second in that race, each more dead than alive. It was third time lucky for me, but it was lucky for Walter in a way, for it was his first " place " in an International event.

Curiously enough, it was the " 250 " Belgian, too, which gave him his first win—it was the following year (1923) and four-strokes were becoming more reliable. Also, Walter had learnt to do more than ride; he had learnt to drive. It was a massed-start race, of course, and he knew that he had the faster machine of the two, whilst he also knew that mine was the more reliable. So, with what must have been, to him, immense restraint, he rode alongside me for eighteen of the twenty laps. Side by side we roared along, laughing at each other and passing flippant (unheard) remarks. At each corner he politely withdrew to give me way, and after it he unobtrusively came back to his place. Two laps from the end he waved me good-bye, tucked himself down in that inimitable style and swiftly departed. Doing all I knew, I finished a couple of minutes behind him, arriving in time to catch his woeful expression whilst in receipt of the bearded kisses which were a penalty of success in the event.

What a race it was! Between us we had set such a pace that we were both faster than the second " 500 " and all the " 350's." Walter, on a " 250," had made second best speed of the day.

That race was the first of his successes, though it was not until 1925 that he had his first T.T. wins, in both the Junior and the Ultra-lightweight. Walter on a " 175 "—oh, the waste of it! I was getting on towards being an " old-stager " in those days, mingling with the Press, the trade representatives, the managing directors. They said, " Oh, young Wal Handley—yes, he's all right on the small stuff!" Somehow the fact that he had won the " Baby " race seemed to detract from his success in the Junior. Some of us, including " Castrol " Andy, said: " He's superb. He's the finest rider the Island has ever seen." (And that was when Alec Bennett was at the height of his well-earned fame). "Shucks," they said, "he'd fall off anything fast." How right they were, for at one time or another he fell off most things! But how little they knew that that was because he was always prepared to try a corner five m.p.h. faster than anyone else! Next year they were confounded.

I have always thought that the 1926 Senior T.T. was Walter's finest race. He was mounted on a twin-cylinder Rex-Acme, which in practice had shown no form at all.

At the end of the first lap he was running second. During that lap he had a minor breakdown which put him back to about 25th. I was on Bray Hill when he descended it at the beginning of the third lap, and the sight of him nearly made my heart stop. It was just staggering. But he was past and gone, and by the time I had walked back to the pits he was signalled at Kirkmichael. Lap after lap he kept up that meteoric pace, overhauling the world's best riders on the world's best machines, until finally he ran into second place. Allowing for his stop, he was some five minutes faster than the winner, this lad who "was all right on the small stuff."

I could give countless other examples of his brilliance as a rider, of the morose, almost sullen way in which he would start a race, and of his gaiety whether winning or losing— when sheer high speed came as a relief to his restless soul. That incredible ride of his on the F.N. from the start to Quarter Bridge, where the model disintegrated, was historic in its hectic briefness—but the crowd thought that he had returned in a huff. That "Belgian" where, in his youthful enthusiasm he couldn't bear to lose sight of his pal Jim Whalley (though he was on a "250" and Jim on a "500"), and where he proved to his own dissatisfaction that wooden railings are unsuitable as banking. Those Montlhéry records which stood for eight years, that wonderful T.T. practice lap when his model behaved more like a buck-jumper than a motor cycle . . . oh, and so many others!

In every race, Walter was the unknown quantity. No matter what contraption he was riding, no matter how apparently small his chances, whilst he was still running there was always the possibility that he might win. Often he would not start if he knew his mount to be unfit, and sometimes he would retire rather than flog a weary motor in a hopeless case. But if he started and was running anywhere in the picture at all, then came the fireworks! He was not so much the crowd's idol as the crowd's thrill.

When I gave up motor cycle racing myself and when Walter was living mainly on the Continent, we naturally saw little of each other, and it was not until I had the temerity, some ten years ago, to learn to fly that we became close friends.

One day I called in to see him at his motor cycle showrooms and suggested a week's flying holiday abroad. He said, "Ah, O.K.!" We set off two days later, and after many minor adventures landed on the triangular piece of grass which in those days was called the Nice aerodrome. After many more adventures, we at last reached Le Bourget, Paris, on our way home, in a full gale. When I set my foot on the tarmac I would cheerfully have sold the machine for the price of the fare home by train and boat, for the last part of the trip had not been ordinary, to say the least of it. But after a few minutes in the buffet we saw "Heracles"— Imperial Airways' 40-passenger liner, the largest and heaviest in the world at that time—come in and land. Walter finished his drink and said: " Are you ready? If that packet can fly, we can." It was no use arguing—he was set for home. We made it—just; but it took six men to hold us to the floor at Lympne, where the Met. officer told us that the wind was gusting up to 73 m.p.h.

He certainly saved my life once, in the air. We were flying a twin-engined monoplane I had just acquired, and when doing a left-hand circuit of the airfield before landing, with the left wing properly down, the left engine stopped. In a flash we were in a power spin, at about 300ft. only. He snapped the throttles back and said, quite casually, "All right, Geoff, I've got her," and fetched her out of the spin with about 20ft. to spare.

Any danger, in any element, was zest to him. He was with me on my boat in Milford Haven once when there was a decent gale blowing. He and I were in the wheelhouse, with others of the party (some rather queasy) below. He was at the wheel. He looked towards the open sea, where the real stuff was to be found, with a questioning glance. I nodded, for I knew my boat, and enjoyed that sort of thing. We headed for the ocean.

He had never handled a boat of that size before, yet it was obvious that he was completely master of her. Pitching and rolling we staggered on, and as we ran into big seas he eased the throttle. Automatically, instinctively, he knew just how much a "machine," be it motor cycle, car, aircraft or boat, could stand without stress. As we hung on by our eyebrows we laughed at each other, just as we had laughed in the Belgian Grand Prix some 15 years before. But when cries for pity reached us from the passengers below, he growled a curse, assumed the customary Handley scowl and turned her about through heavy waves—a tricky job—as if he had been handling her for years.

It was his superb judgment which made him supreme on the road, whether on two wheels for four, and in the air, with any craft from D.H. Moth to Short Stirling. Yet he was always willing to exceed that judgment, knowing that he was doing so. He crashed more often than anyone I have known, usually because he was prepared to take the extra risk and chance the impossible. His quickness of thought and action was incredible, and early in his career he had reduced high-speed crashing to a fine art. As Dougal Marchant—his colleague and racing manager at the time (as far as he would let anyone manage him)—once said, " If Walter didn't know how to fall off he'd have been killed a hundred times."

Yet with all his abilities in this direction he had many nasty accidents. In his time he broke many bones, including his back, and finished with a fractured base of the skull. Yet none of these accidents affected his nerve, his physical power, or his mental alertness. Only the fractured base troubled him at all, and that because it robbed him of his sense of smell.

Walter was a man with many friends and only one real enemy—himself. He would have had far more success in life had he been less morose in manner, less bluntly and directly accusing when ill-used. Many fine qualities he had, but not tact.

Most of those who knew of him, but did not know him, thought him a rider and driver, pure and simple. But he was far more than that. Whilst not a qualified engineer, or actual designer, he invariably knew what was wrong with a machine and what would put it right—a faculty denied to most accredited designers. He was in addition an astute business man, and could spot flaws in a balance sheet as quickly as a chartered accountant.

The last time I met him we were mourning the death of Amy Johnson, whom we both knew well. Now Walter himself has gone. How or where he died I do not know, for I am stationed in a place where news is slow and scarce. But of this I am certain. That he died through no fault or misjudgment of his own and that he fought to the last to save himself and his machine; for the care of his craft was always foremost in his mind.

It was often said, " A race without Walter is like an egg without salt." Now it must be said, " A world without Walter is a poorer world indeed." Whilst his friends live, he will never be forgotten.

On New Year's Day, 1942, the Editor of "The Motor Cycle" received the following letter from an eye-witness of the crash which resulted in Walter's death:

Kirkbride,
Carlisle.

Dear Sir,

Mr. Davison, in his article in appreciation of the late W. L. Handley, makes a plea for some information about his crash. Perhaps a few remarks of mine may help him to make a few deductions. Walter took off from an aerodrome situated near the above address and crashed in a ploughed field within five minutes of being air-borne. He was piloting an Aira-Cobra. When he took off, the motor was "moving" hard, making an awful din and when he throttled down, it appeared to cut out, then spluttered for a few seconds and finally died out. Wal side-slipped towards a wood with, it seemed, the intention of putting his craft into the tree tops. He missed this wood by feet. The starboard wing hit the ground first and the machine immediately exploded.

Yours faithfully,
P. W. BULMAN.

Recently, I met another eye-witness—Mr. J. W. Holt, who was employed at Kirkbride aerodrome at the time. He told me that Walter's actual take-off was perfect, and that he at once got the machine into a nice, steady climb. This must have been a few seconds before the development of the mechanical trouble, referred to by Mr. Bulman.

G.S.D.

SOME ANIMAL ANTICS
By Eric Briggs.

The most amusing incident I recall was during practice for the 1947 Clubman's T.T. Approaching Ramsey at a fair speed, two dogs appeared from nowhere, and for what seemed quite a long time ran alongside me. After various remarks made by people as to the capabilities of "Clubmen" and their steeds, this incident seemed the final blow to our pride! However, it was some consolation that there was no-one about to witness and recount this " race," which I am glad to say I won, the dogs eventually retiring, apparently to wait for the next Clubman!

One of my most hectic moments also occurred during practising for the Clubman's. Just after the S-bend outside Kirkmichael village there is a slight rise and then a drop down to the very fast right sweep leading to the Bishop's Court. I was going up this rise, from which the drop is " blind," and as I topped it I was greeted with the sight of five or six cows all over the road! There seemed only one way through—stopping was out of the question—and that was between the sharp end of one and the blunt end of another! Thanks to their good sense in keeping still, this was accomplished, though I swear to this day that my elbow grazed the snout of the sharp-ended one, as it was in the act of mooing. (I reported the cows to the next marshall). Truly it was a most anxious moment.

Further animal incidents crop up in my mind, though they are not quite so hectic as that one. During the actual Clubman's race a hen tried suicide at the same spot—it failed. And at the Laurel Bank there were some sheep, or maybe they were goats, on the road. Then during practice for the 1938 Manx there was the hare at the bottom of Bray Hill, which on two mornings running tried racing with a 490 c.c. Manx Norton! And in the practising for the '46 Manx, I was charging round the " Verandah " when a black rabbit suddenly jumped off the bank as I was passing and frightened the life out of me!

HE DIDN'T WANT A CLOSE-UP

By JOHNNIE LOCKETT.

I always remember the second lap of the Senior Manx in 1938. It was a beautiful day, and I was cracking along, full of the joy of Spring. At the second Mountain Box, i.e. the left-hander after the Bungalow, there was a spectator intent on taking photographs, and leaning on the wire fence.

Unknown to me, the oil tank had sprunk a leak a few miles back and oil had been splashing on the rear tyre. The first indication I got was when the rear wheel endeavoured to catch up with the front one on this bend. I was fairly occupied in trying to sort things out, but I shall never forget the look of astonishment on the photographer's face and his terrific leap for safety. The leaking oil tank held enough to take me to the pit stop, but I often wondered if the photographer got his picture!

TRIAL AND TRIBULATION
By Allan Jefferies.

The occasion on which I came nearest to being, to put it mildly, flurried, was on the fifth day of the 1936 International Six Days, in the Bavarian Alps. I had just passed the finish of one of the many timed hill climbs when the motor cut out completely. I hurriedly changed a plug, and still no response. A new contact-breaker was fitted without any improvement. The carburetter jet was then detached and the needle fell out, indicating a broken clip.

Time was pressing, so I refitted the jet and decided to fit the needle after the next time-check. As I was in danger of being late at the next check I really pressed the loud pedal, after placing the needle in a safe place—to wit, my mouth. The path was somewhat mountainous, and a drainage system consisting of logs of wood placed diagonally across the road made motoring uncomfortable and fast motoring suicidal. Anyway, I bought a lovely box of tacks when the bike overturned owing to the front wheel refusing to jump one of the wooden gullies.

I rushed back to the bike after I picked myself up, and discovered the throttle outer cable severely distorted, causing the engine to sound like a million r.p.m., and the foot change assembly smashed off the gearbox. I got to the check on time, but I don't know how. Red Cross attendants grabbed me at sight, owing to the fact that I was absolutely plastered with blood. I then found out that the carb. needle was missing, but it had left a memento in a badly torn mouth. In addition, the index finger of my right hand was very deeply cut, and I was aware that I was bruised all over.

The final check of the day was reached without loss of marks, but I was in pretty bad shape. Some very sporting British spectators made the 50-mile trip to Fussen, where some International Motor Cyclists Touring Club chaps were staying, and borrowed a foot change assembly from another Triumph. This I fitted on my bike in the fifteen minutes allowed next morning, then at the first check I fitted a new throttle cable, carburetter needle and clip, just in time to attack the last speed hill climb of the week.

The trial finished at lunch time except for the one-hour speed test in the afternoon. I was in the British Vase Team with Len Heath and Jack Williams, and although I qualified for a gold medal we were unsuccessful in our attempt to win the Vase, owing, I think, to my inability to use the front brake, as my right hand was so badly damaged. Never was I more pleased to finish an event!

THORNS IN THE FLESH
By Eric Williams.

May, 1914, seems a long way back now, but we had our thrills and spills; and they were just as exciting as those of the modern competitor, with his maximum something over a hundred against ours of something over a mile a minute. Remember that we had stirrup front brakes—to comply with the law!—side valves, $2\frac{1}{4}$ inch tyres and high frames. However, I always prided myself on not suffering from gravel-rash; in fact, it was thorns in the posterior on this occasion!

It was midway through practising in that year of peace and plenty. The oil Barons waited on competitors in any open event with their respective green red, brown and gilded tins, to fill or top you up before you could as much as bat an eyelid—and paid you a bonus to allow them to do it!

But back to that particular practice run. On my second

lap on this glorious May morning, I was making a fast trip round when near Kirkmichael I caught up a well-known rider on a Senior Rover. He was undoubtedly unaware of my presence, but I could see that my line was clear to overtake, when—suddenly—his rear mudguard was against my front wheel! I have a hazy recollection of going sky-high and landing on my back on top of a wide strong hedge, with nothing more amiss than a few pricks from the thorns. I was on my legs in a minute, inspecting the model, which had a damaged front wheel and fork girder. The Manx Railway was the transport back, and the Managers and team were much relieved to find I was in one piece.

DROPPING THE PILOT

BY C. W. (PADDY) JOHNSTON.

In 1921 Stanley Woods and I went to the Island to have a look at this great race. I had my Harley-Davidson 1000 c.c. solo with me.

A friend of ours who said he knew the way round offered to be our guide, so off we set, I driving and Stanley behind me, and behind him our friend.

Very soon after starting George, our friend, called out, " Slow down! Here's Ramsey Hairpin!" He did this about a dozen times before we actually reached the Hairpin, and by then both Stanley and I were a bit fed up—you can cry Wolf too often. However, when we did reach the Hairpin we got round in very nice style and the getaway was really good, even for a 1,000 c.c. I remarked as much to Stanley, who answered very calmly, " Yes, we dropped George at the Hairpin."

As a point of interest re that same lap—we did it in 58 minutes, and had to open and shut the Mountain gates as well.

During the 1922 practising (my first year of T.T. riding) I was coming down to Craig-ny-baa on my 250 New Imp., when Len Horton, also riding a New Imp., came up alongside.

Determined not to give way I kept the throttle open long past what I considered the safety margin and got into the bend slightly ahead of Len. But when I did try to brake, imagine my horror when I found that the rear brake rod was somewhere on the Mountain!—and the front brake in those days was more or less an ornament. By doing a quick hand change from top to bottom, zigzagging all across the road, I managed to get round, but that was the one and only time I remember when my hair seemed to stand straight up with fright. I had hair in those days!

Then there was one hectic moment on Ballaugh Bridge. During practising for the 1923 T.T. Stanley and I were having a " do "—lots of dust and the sun straight in our eyes. Stanley was leading and I was close behind. Someone else was about 200 yards in front of Stanley, and visibility was nil owing to dust. Suddenly Stanley and I became airborne, very high indeed, and the next second we were rubbing the ends of our handlebars on the wall just past the Bridge. Never again, I hope!

When I was on my fifth lap in the 1925 Lightweight, the bolt which holds the front mudguard on the top end of the forks fell out. All the way round the mudguard kept swinging backwards and forwards, ready at any moment to swing right under the wheel. Remembering the same thing happening to Jimmy Shaw some years earlier, with very unpleasant results, I didn't feel happy. All through the last lap it got worse and worse, but I just got over the line to finish second. When the machine was being pushed into the Paddock, the mudguard swung right under the wheel—lucky escape!

The Brooklands 200, 1923. After 50 miles I saw a dark mass near the mile box, and ran slap into it. Yes, a beautiful swarm of bees . . . . Being a very hot day, I was riding " light " and I got the full effects of them, down my shirt front, up my arms, down my neck. By the finish I was a white mass of blisters. Nasty. Very nasty.

I SHOWED 'EM ROUND

By BERTIE ROWELL.

Having driven an Official Car from 1925 to 1929, and there being no prospect of racing a bike on the course, I persuaded the Chief Marshal in September, 1930, that I was a suitable person to be a " pilot " for the newcomers, and on the first practice morning I arrived at the start with my 1924 Sunbeam.

The first " beginner " allocated to me was Jock Forbes, whom I knew. When he saw the bicycle he had a chat about a waste of time and set off without me. Eventually I was given six riders to look after, including Freddie Frith, Bert Parrish and, I believe, Harold Daniell. There was a near riot, and I was informed in no uncertain terms that I had better get a red move on.

By this time I quite regretted being mixed up in the affair at all, but I set off as fast as the Sunbeam would go— probably about the 70 mark as a maximum—and what happened from then on I only heard afterwards. Two of them went up the Castletown Road at Quarter Bridge and another two left the party at Braddan. Freddie told me afterwards that all was going well with him until without warning I turned sharp right up what looked to him like a farm lane, but which he found afterwards was the course beyond Balla-craine. He went straight on towards Peel, but he soon discovered his mistake, turned round, and caught me up in Glen Helen.

On Creg Willys Daniell passed, but stopped shortly after with some bother.

Passing the Stonebreaker's Hut just before the Snaefell Shoulder I saw Jock Forbes being looked after by the Marshal. He had come off and damaged his ankle—and next day he told me he might have been better off following me(!). On return to the start Freddie Frith's time was recorded as 40—0. None of the others of the group were near this time.

A newspaper reported from Quarter Bridge that the most

alarming incident was the arrival of an un-numbered rider on what they described as a " pre-saddle-tank Sunbeam," at a very dangerous speed, followed by several riders, two of whom took the slip road, and similar remarks came from various points, Union Mills declaring the un-numbered Sunbeam to be the fastest machine of the morning. I still have the cutting. As far as I remember, I 'phoned the Chief Marshal and told him I would not be available for any future mornings—which may have saved him some bother.

I should add that the Chief Marshals since that time have profited from this experience, and such matters are now conducted with much more decorum. I have even recently been entrusted with the job of piloting people round the Course, mostly to their satisfaction, although it may be remembered that last September I had to leave one " pupil " on the Mountain, who subsequently disappeared for three days. When he was found, a certain mainland Daily came out with the headline " I went to Peel with a Red-Head." He did, too.

A JOKE WITH A LUCKY BREAK
By Fred Dixon.

My win in the 1923 Sidecar T.T. rather stands out in my memory as a kind of joke with a lucky break in it.

Having arranged to ride a Douglas outfit in this race, I thought I had better get down to the factory in Bristol to see what sort of a job was being prepared. I found they were busy making up a job with a leaning body, and I didn't much care for it. As there was only about a week before we must leave for the Island I was quite a bit worried, and after one or two sleepless nights I dreamt of that comic thing the " banking sidecar."

It seemed a hopeless proposition to get one made up in time, but I thought " nothing venture—nothing gain," and promptly turned my sex appeal on to Bill Bailey, who was in charge at the time. He laughed when I mooted the idea of getting one through in time, but I eventually persuaded him that it might be done and he placed the whole resources of the factory at my disposal.

There was no time for drawings, so I did a quick bit of chalking on the Experimental Shop floor, and with a few willing helpers, and not bothering about sleep, we knocked up a complete sidecar with an all-metal body having a rolling seat, as used by some oarsmen. Nothing needed modification, and my first passenger — the one and only Alec Bennett—was enthusiastic at the tricks we could get up to.

We landed in the Isle of Man feeling very happy, but had a nasty shock when the scrutineers put the bar up and said we could not use such a dangerous contraption, and during the early practice period we had to have the works locked in the rigid position. However, my pleading availed, and we were allowed to use the gadget for one lap under close observation at different parts of the course. The job worked fine, and we carved quite a chunk off the lap record with my passenger, young Walter Denny, sitting in a perfectly normal manner.

The day of the race came with things looking very rosy, and off we went. We very quickly passed those who had started before us. As it appeared we had so much in hand, I eased up considerably, and Denny and I entertained each other up the Mountain singing " We Won't be Home Till Morning."

A shock was coming, for I had forgotten those behind, and suddenly there was a nasty scream and Harry Langman passed us. Mental calculation told me that we would really have to get our skates on now. Up went the wick, and I soon repassed him, not knowing whether he would need to stop for fuel, as we must do. I got that job over, and was just pushing off when Harry came chasing through. He led me towards Braddan Bridge, and we arrived there some two seconds later to find him upside down and sliding all over the place. We missed him, but I don't know to this day how it was done.

Breathing a sigh of relief, I kept the steam on, thinking there might be others I had miscalculated. More trouble was brewing, for as we took Hilberry on this—the last—lap, at somewhat hectic speed, the inner duplex frame tube suddenly snapped. The handlebar jamming on the body top stopped a total collapse, but it was only by wangling the banking lever that we were able to hobble home and see the welcome chequered flag.

Sorry, Harry, you should have won—but you did it yourself. Naughty, naughty!

LEARNING THE WAY ROUND
By Bill McVeigh.

I began racing in 1945, at an age when most intelligent individuals have retired from the sport, and the 1946 M.G.P. was my first real road race. Incidentally I had never before been to the Isle of Man, so my first problems were to find which way round the race was run, the route, the names and positions of all the famous " hazards " and how to take them quickly in the highest gear without losing revs or road. Loss of either has no future in it on a megaphone racer!

I blew two Junior engines during Practice—very expensive —and in the Junior race had a miserable run as far as Cregny-Baa, where a solid engine on the corner gave me plenty to think about for a few hectic seconds which seemed like years. However, I eventually found the elusive clutch lever and coasted to a safe area. I did enjoy watching how the good riders took the bend—I also enjoyed the kindly Marshal's sandwiches! They're grand people, these M.G.P. folks.

In the Senior race I finished 15th after numerous stops on the Mountain, swearing I'd have no more to do with racing. I shall never forget those awful weather conditions, when the black dye soaked out of my leathers and turned my shirt, vest and skin black from neck to knees. I only carried on for the sake of my team-mates H. Clark and D. Tynan, both of whom told me they had only finished for the same reason—

something in this Team business! The last three laps I rode without goggles, and either because of failing eyesight, due to the huge raindrops, or through inexperience of the course, I took the straight-on route twice at Ballacraine. I expect the Marshals thought I was crazy! Also on one occasion during this race I forgot that Signpost had a right turn. Still, I did finish intact, and if Eric Briggs hadn't been so darn persistent after his involuntary stop in Ramsey our team would have won the team prize!

I entered the Clubman's Lightweight T.T. in 1947 to learn the course better. Many stretches were still "foreign territory" to me. Practising for this race on the 250 Triumph and the actual race itself were the happiest memories I have of the T.T. course. Nothing I have yet ridden handled so well as this little standard production machine—perfect steering and an engine which never missed a beat. I decided to put in the minimum number of practice laps, to ensure the engine being in good trim for the race, for frankly I didn't think an engine which was never intended for racing would stand up to a lot of caning. I know better now!

My only spares in the Island for this machine (which was last produced in 1939) were one exhaust valve, two valve springs and a set of clutch plates. In reply to my enquiry for spare piston rings, Mr. Wellworthy told me he could not help with rings for a 0.20 piston, so I just had to be careful. I need hardly remark further on the difficulties in which this same oversize piston involved me after winning the race at 65.30 m.p.h. However, thanks to the loyalty and untiring efforts of that grand body of sportsmen, the Derby Pathfinders Club, and their able secretary Arthur Taylor, we eventually received the Handley Trophy and cash awards, together with costs against the A-C.U. Stewards. This was the decision of the R.A.C. Appeals Committee on the evidence placed before them.

The 1947 M.G.P. gave me my best times round the Course, and in the Senior I got my first replica, finishing sixth. I was

also a member of the winning team, with Charles Salt and
C. H. Francis. This race lives in my memory as the one in
which I took the most risks. My last lap was a nightmare of
skids, for unknown to me the front crankcase oil-breather
pipe had sheared and the front wheel and tyre were covered
in oil. Taking the 33rd full bore in top gear I felt the bike
slip slightly sideways. I thought this might be due to an
eddy of wind, but later at the Creg I found it was no such
thing—first the front wheel skidded, then round came the
rear wheel and I smacked the bank about half a dozen times.
I just couldn't seem to get away from it, until with arms and
legs working like a windmill I managed to kick clear and
resume my flight to the finish, a very shaken rider!

A PACKET OF TROUBLES

BY BEN DRINKWATER.

In 1937 I decided to have a bash at the Manx Grand Prix.
I scratched up all the pennies I could and purchased an old
Excelsior Manxman. It had already had its time, but it was
the best I could do.

I started off by dropping a valve on the first morning's
practice, which messed the motor up a bit. There were no
Excelsior representatives over then, so I was going round like
a millionaire who had lost all his money until the Thursday,
when a real sportsman named F. Cadman offered me the loan
of his hack bike to get my practice laps in. I still had three
laps to do to qualify, and three days to do them in. It looked
like a piece of cake, but my troubles weren't over. I put in
a nice quiet lap on Friday morning, and I got my own machine back in the afternoon and took it out on the Saturday.
I used a gallon of oil in 26 miles and then seized up, so I still
had two laps to do, and only one day left.

The Excelsior was ready for battle again at 10 p.m. on the
Sunday night. I don't think I slept that night, but I was up
bright and early the next morning. I received kind advice
from the boys, and then set off for practice, but I didn't get

far because a bright young fellow with an M.G. was having a race with himself and knocked the back end of my bike from under me, smashing the gearbox. F. Cadman's hack bike came to the rescue again, and I just managed to qualify —but that's about all I did in 1937. The machine used another gallon of oil in a lap, and I packed up, a tired and broke man. I came back with twopence in my pocket, and owing Excelsiors a fiver!

Here are just a few details of other races I have been in. In 1938 I finished sixth with a very soft back tyre, which made cornering very difficult. In 1946, but for that oil leak that started on the very first lap I should probably have won: as it was I couldn't keep my feet on the rests, they were so slippery.

In the 1947 North West 200 I was nicely in the lead, and then it started to rain and I got water in the electrics and limped home second.

When I started in the 1947 T.T. I hoped I had had my share of bad luck and was expecting to get in third place, but Mr. Bad Luck gave me another dig: I cooked a plug at the Gooseneck, and I thought I'd had it again, because by the look of the gradient it seemed as though I would never restart the machine. However, I had a go, and it started on the second attempt. I can tell you I had to have a breather after the first effort, and I thought I hadn't any lungs left after the second!

All this may seem to suggest that my middle name is hard luck, but that's how it is. I haven't yet had a trouble-free run in all my races—but here's hoping!

I BLUSH TO REMEMBER
By Charlie Collier.

The following experience happened before the present generation of readers and riders were born, but it was the most embarrassing incident of my racing career and it taught me a lesson I never forgot.

Shortly after passing Union Mills on the third lap of the

1911 T.T., I found myself, for some mysterious reason, practically out of petrol. In those days filling was permitted at Ramsey as well as at the start, and having decided from practice consumption that my machine could easily complete three laps on one fill, I had thought I would play safe and fill at Ramsey on the third circuit. Instead, I found my tank almost dry shortly after completing two laps.

By continually stopping, blowing into and shaking the tank to fill the float chamber, I was eventually able to make Balla-craine, where a kindly marshall found me sufficient petrol to carry on to Ramsey—but I'd lost in all well over ten minutes. However, in the last lap I managed to regain the lead . . . and then only a mile or so from the finish I had the misfortune to puncture the rear tyre. Since riding on the rim was out of the question in those days of beaded edge tyres, I had perforce to stop once more and pump up, just managing to reach the finish before I was again on the rim—only to find that after having had twelve stops in all I was 63 seconds behind the winner, O. C. Godfrey, on a foreign make of machine for the first time. To add to my mortification and embarrassment, I was subsequently disqualified for having taken in petrol at an unauthorized place. Why my consumption in the actual race was so much higher than in practice, I was never able to determine.

Of hectic experiences I had plenty, but I think the most hectic of all happened way back in 1906 during a series of needle-match races on Canning Town cycle track, with G. A Barnes, the keenest rival I ever had on these small three-laps-to-a-mile tracks. In one of these matches I covered a flying mile in 57.4/5 seconds—62 m.p.h. This may sound a ridiculous speed in these days, but it nevertheless constituted an unbeatable record, for it represented just about the very limit of tyre adhesion on the inadequate bankings of the track, designed, as they were, for pedal cycling.

Anyhow, it was certainly the most foolhardy feat I ever accomplished, and although the race (three miles, standing start) only occupied a trifle over three minutes, those minutes were hectic enough while they lasted—so much so that I did not know until afterwards that my rival had retired during the event. It may be of interest to record that the machine I used was a 7 h.p. twin, weighing, complete with pedalling gear, under 110 lbs., the specified weight limit for International racing machines at that time.

REVENGE

By Albert Moule.

There was an occasion during practising for the 1946 Manx that I really enjoyed. I was out on my 350 c.c. one morning, moving fairly quickly on the Mountain, when I realized I was being tailed. I proceeded to try and lose my shadow, but no—it couldn't be done. We passed the Bungalow and Windy Corner, and on the approach to the 33rd we overtook another rider. Whilst I was hesitating about which side to pass him, the man I had been trying to shake off passed both of us. I didn't mind this too much, but what I didn't like was being hit smack on the nose by a large stone thrown up by his rear wheel.

That did it. I went after him! We tore round the 33rd, Keppel and Kate's Cottage, and down to the Creg, and by this time I had realized that the fellow certainly could go. I was now close enough to recognize Ken Bills as the rider, which made me more determined than ever to pass him. I watched and waited, and synchronised my gear changing with Ken's (I don't think he realized that I was still with him) and as we came out of Brandish I left my gear-change just a fraction later—and just managed to squeeze by at Hilberry.

I thought at the time " That's for hitting me on the nose!" and later I was still more satisfied on seeing by the times that Ken had made best time of the morning in the 350 class. Yet I had overtaken him! That was a really enjoyable moment.

A BIT SHEEPISH

By Howard Davies.

My funniest recollection in connection with the T.T. is of an incident during the practising period in 1920, the first post-that-war race year.

I was riding for A.J.S., and owing to a most unfortunate series of accidents to the team during practice we had used up all the reserve men and had to indent for more to come over to the Island from the works to take their places. Two or three of the casualties we had suffered were the result of collisions with straying sheep on the Mountain road, mainly due to the foggy conditions which prevailed that year in the early mornings—and in consequence we were all a bit " sheep conscious," no doubt.

One morning I was motoring up the Mountain as fast as the foggy conditions would permit, and I began to overhaul another rider who turned out, when I got close enough to identify him, to be one of the reserve riders who had come over to replace a casualty.

I knew him for a cheery fellow who had a very good sense of humour, so I edged my way closer and closer to him until I got within a few yards of his tail, when I let out a terrific " BA-A-A-A-A!" I could see by the way he shuddered that the noise had registered with him, so I proceeded to repeat it at frequent intervals, and each time he heard it he shuddered a bit more and crouched lower over his handlebars, opening the taps to try and escape the harrowing noise. This process went on until finally he plucked up courage to look round and see what it was all about: when he saw me right on his tail he gave a sickly grin, brandished his fist at me and disappeared in the mist.

When we returned to the pits at the end of the lap he made a bee-line for me in the coffee tent, and after a spot of leg-pull I asked him what his reactions were. He said he was scared stiff at the first bleat, but when the bleats continued to gain on him he was absolutely petrified, and said to himself, " By God, I've had a bit to do with sheep in my time, but I never thought one could travel as fast as a racing A.J.S.!"

I MISTOOK THE SIGNAL
By F. W. Fry.

I am still kicking myself for the mistake I made in the 1947 Junior T.T., when I misunderstood the meaning of my pit signal. Although I didn't know it, I was lying fourth on the first and second laps, and when they signalled " 4 " from the pit I took it to mean that I was only four seconds inside replica time. This notion shook me considerably, and I went all out to improve what I thought was a bad state of affairs —with the sad consequence that in my frantic attempts to do better I went through the hedge at Handley's Corner.

You can imagine my feelings when I arrived at a nearby farmhouse just in time to hear Graham Walker announce over the radio that " F. W. Fry is lying fourth at the end of the second lap "!

HOW GREEN WAS OUR STANLEY
By H. F. Brockbank.

Stanley Woods has so often explained that in his first T.T. he was absolutely green in all matters mechanical that I am sure he will not mind me narrating the following true story.

In 1922 the Cotton team consisted of myself, Freddy Morgan, the Cotton works manager, and a young enthusiast named Stanley Woods. We had no mechanics, and the bikes arrived very late; and there was a lot of work to be done on them, as Stanley has mentioned in his " Reminiscences." With an hour to go before the bikes had to be handed in to the Stewards, Freddy and I were working frantically to make up new gear lever spindles, while Stanley wrapped insulation tape round every conceivable part of his mount—Freddy and I hadn't time to do this to ours.

Desperately, I handed Stanley a bar of steel I had managed to scrounge and told him to saw it into three lengths. A few strokes—and, of course, bang went the hacksaw blade! I gave him my last saw blade, with dire threats as to what would happen if he broke it. I watched him make a few strokes, and noticed that he had put the blade in the frame the wrong way. Impatiently I pointed out his mistake, and I was completely shattered by his reply:

" Now Brock," said Stanley, reproachfully, " I know I'm green, but I'm not so green as all that. I know all about your buckets of steam and your left-handed screwdrivers and all the other things you kid new apprentices with, but you can't kid me that a hacksaw blade has a top and a bottom!"

IT MIGHT HAVE BEEN DIFFERENT
By Geoff Davison.

[*Reproduced by courtesy of " Motor Cycling " in which paper this article appeared on 7th October, 1943*]

"IT might have been different . . . " There are many other titles I could have given this tale—" The Plot That Failed," " The Irony of Fate," and so on, but the one I have chosen seems to deal the nail the shrewdest blow. It might have been different—

Each one of us, of course, can look back to something which has changed his motorcycling life. Many of us can point to occurrences, tiny in themselves, which influenced not only our own lives, but those of many others. I personally can recall two things which, coming one after the other nearly 20 years ago, altered the whole of my career and, perhaps, the fortunes of a firm of manufacturers. They were " Little Roger's Failure " and " The Affair of the Black Paint."

A dab of black paint—well, say two or three small brushfuls! Applied in 1924, in the right place, they might have won a T.T. race and might have turned a small firm into a large and very prosperous one; and myself into a substantial Birmingham manufacturer instead of an elderly soldier sweating in an African sun. A dab of black paint! It might have been different—

Well, here's the story. Just after the last war, the fortunes of motorcycle firms were being made or marred by racing. One of the firms was Levis, for which I was riding. In 1920 a two-stroke Levis in the hands of R. O. Clark won the Lightweight Class of the Junior T.T. The following year a Levis was second in the same race and in 1922, Levis-mounted, I won the first real Lightweight T.T. This was followed by successes in the French and Belgian Grands Prix and in the International Six Days' Trial of the same year— a record of which any firm might well be proud. The post-war slump was beginning and many mushroom firms had died. But, in a small way, Levis sales were good.

It soon became apparent, however, that a major decision must be made. Either the firm must rest on its laurels and be content to go on in a small way or it must repeat its racing successes and prove that the two-stroke was equal or superior to its four-stroke opponent. The battle of two-stroke versus four-stroke was at its height. To withdraw was to admit defeat; to continue meant new designs, for the four-strokes were getting faster and more reliable. The Butterfield brothers and Bob Newey, directors of the Levis concern, decided to carry on the fight. I was all in favour of it.

With the approach of the winter of 1922, Bob Newey put on his thinking cap. He was the designer of the firm and he it was who had personally made my winning 1922 Lightweight T.T. engine. But he realized that the engine represented very nearly the limit of efficiency in straightforward two-stroke design. Not quite the limit, for he knew he could make an engine just as reliable and a shade faster, as in fact he did, too late, the following year. But he was aware that such an engine could not compete indefinitely with the ever-increasing speeds which the four-strokes were showing. There must be drastic changes in design.

He broke his news to me in December, '22, during one of the many ham-roll lunches when we talked racing shop in his little greenhouse of an office. He was building me a supercharged two-stroke engine for the 1923 T.T.!

Naturally my enthusiasm knew no bounds. A supercharged T.T. engine, twenty years ago! After so comfortable a win with a normal engine in the 1922 race, a supercharged edition seemed a certain winner for the next event. Newey designed by intuition, not slide-rule and test-bench. He was certain it would work, and he had never yet been wrong. The prospect was indeed rosy.

Slowly but surely the supercharged Levis engine was designed and made. We called it " Little Roger," for it was so distinctive and hush-hush an engine that it needed a "nom-de-sport." The word " supercharger " was banned from our thoughts and words—my coming engine was 'Little Roger' to everyone. None of the many factory representatives who were called in to provide special metals, stampings, piston rings and the like, knew that we were planning a supercharged engine. They supplied the bits and pieces for " Little Roger " and left us, thinking that we were mad. The secret of " Little Roger " was well kept.

I doubt if one word of it has ever appeared in print, so I will give a few brief details. The engine itself was of the normal type, but on the off side of the crankcase was cast a small aluminium cylinder with a bore of about 55 mm. A tiny piston, with a midget connecting rod, was operated from a crank on the off side of the engine shaft, the stroke being, so far as I remember, about 50 mm. This little piston worked in conjunction with the normal piston, sucking more gas into the crankcase and compressing it to a very much higher ratio than ever before. What it amounted to was an additional intake of 55 by 50 mm.—a very considerable increase on the normal 62.5 by 82 mm. And all simplicity itself.

" It won't give you very much more speed," Bob told me. " Perhaps three or four miles an hour. But the acceleration will be colossal."

He never spoke truer words. " Little Roger " was finished and tested early in May, 1923. I took him to the Castle Bromwich straight where, with spies out to warn us of the approach of the police, we carried out preliminary tests. My winning 1922 Levis had had a maximum of 63 m.p.h. and acceleration superior to anything in the race; " Little Roger " clocked 66, and its acceleration was absolutely phenomenal. Never have I ridden anything like it. The main difficulty was staying on the machine when one opened the throttle.

But there was one big snag, and this was the first of those two things which, perhaps, altered the whole of my life. Just as the acceleration was beyond all possible imagination, so was the vibration! I was tough in those days and normal vibration worried me not at all. Many a time R. E. Pugh, one of the Levis testers, would come back with a machine and say, " Vibration's chronic." " Go on, you're soft," I would reply, and prove that vibration didn't worry *me*. But the vibration of " Little Roger," like the Biblical peace, passed all understanding. In two runs along the Castle Bromwich straight, a mile each way, I wore out the palms and thumbs of a pair of gloves, and hanging on to the bars was like holding those high-voltage electric shock machines which one patronizes at Fun Fairs. I began to think that I would have a rough ride in the T.T.

I reported to Bob. He knew that if I complained of vibration, it was no ordinary vibration. And he knew in a flash that " Little Roger " was a failure. As usual, he lit a cigarette before replying. Then he said:

" We ought to have balanced the blower piston, Dave, but it's such a tiddling little thing that I didn't think it would need it. It's too late now. Still, you'd better try it out on the track."

belt! A belt can stand much harsher treatment than chains and shock absorbers. At least, so I thought.

Day after day I went out, and day after day we dismantled the engine, trued up the shaft and reassembled. On the last Friday of practice I returned to the Peel garage after one lap, alone, with an unholy idea in my head. Could not this distortion, I wondered, be cured by dealing the flywheel rim a terriffic blow in the required direction? Would the crankshaft break under such treatment, would the flywheel burst into a thousand fragments? Well, if it did, I still had my practice engine, which was pretty decent. I was so fed up with stripping that engine day after day that I was prepared to chance it. I figured out which way the flywheel needed bouncing and looked about for a suitable weapon. I soon found one—a 7-lb sledge-hammer with a 3-ft. haft.

After a quick glance round to make sure that I was still alone, I fixed the Levis securely in a corner of the garage, stood back, took a deep breath, grasped the hammer, prayed " mechanically " and dealt that flywheel an eightpenny one. The noise, in the confined space, was like a high-pitched Big Ben tolling one o'clock, but although the Levis shuddered in a frightened sort of way, it settled quickly and before the clamour had subsided I was on my knees checking the fly wheel. It was running dead true!

Hurriedly I replaced the sledge-hammer, dressed up and set off for another lap. That engine ran perfectly, and I put up one of my best practice times. At the end of it the fly-wheel was out of the true as usual, but not more than usual.

When we were all back in the hotel I slipped down to the garage and seized the hammer again. One blow, and all was well. After breakfast there was a mystery. Several mechanics could testify that they had checked the flywheel when I came in, and found it out of true—all very odd. I did not enlighten them, but I told Bob Newey.

There was one more morning to test the finished plan—the acquisition and transport of " a portable apparatus for trueing up crankshafts during T.T. races." This took the form

That evening Pugh and I left for Brooklands, with a car load of frames, wheels and spare parts. Next morning I set off for a few laps, and half-way round the second lap the frame broke, just above the gearbox. This locked the primary chain and, as there was no clutch, the back wheel as well. I was ready for it and, with feet well out, skidded to a stand-still. We fitted " Little Roger " into another frame and I set off again, with the same result. This happened a third and a fourth time and each time I survived. But the average life of a frame that housed " Little Roger " was about five miles!

I 'phoned Bob Newey. " All right, Dave," he said, " I'll get on with your other engine." So we drove back to Birmingham with a car load of frames and buried " Little Roger " beneath the bench in that Holy of Holies, the Levis competition department.

It was just one of those things—one of those two things which made all the difference. And the other was " The Affair of the Black Paint."

After the demise of " Little Roger " we all went to the Isle of Man; that is, all except Bob Newey, who worked like a slave on my other engine. But it was not finished in time for the T.T., and I rode a practice machine and just got a Replica.

The 1923 engine was even better than the " very remarkable two-stroke " (as " Motor Cycling " had described it) that had scored me the Hat Trick the previous year, and it gave me an easy win in the French Grand Prix, and a hard-fought second to Wal Handley in the Belgian race. But it was the T.T. that counted, and we had been also-rans in that. In the autumn of the year there was again a Decision to be made. To race or not to race?

The news that there would be an Ultra-Lightweight race for machines of 175 c.c. capacity settled the matter. We might stand little chance in the " 250," for the four-strokes were getting ever faster and more reliable, and it was un-likely that even a balanced " Little Roger " would be able to compete with them. But the " 175 " event seemed just up our street; in fact, as near a racing certainty as could be anticipated.

In the racing game it is no use splitting your effort, as so many have found. It was a case of developing " Little Roger " or concentrating on a fizzer for the Ultra-Light-weight. " Little Roger " lost the day and remained with an ever-thickening coat of dust and cigarette ash beneath the bench. Bob Newey settled down to the baby engine, and therein lies the story of the black paint.

The " 175 " engine was of the normal three-port design, but with a much higher compression ratio than we had ever used before. Now a high-compression ratio means high in-ternal heat—and the necessity for getting rid of same. In the past our engines had had aluminium jackets and radiating flanges shrunk over the cast-iron cylinders, and these had provided fairly good radiation. But Bob Newey felt that the system would not be adequate for the much higher ratio he proposed using for the " 175 " job. Copper, he decided, with its much superior heat-conducting properties, was the only thing. So the " 175 " engine had copper radiating flanges and, of course, was at once named " Copper-nob."

What an engine that was! Like most other Levis racing engines it was not ready until a few days before the race, but the first day out in practice I knew well that, barring acci-dents, I had the Ultra-Lightweight Trophy in the bag. I shall always remember poor Phil Pike's disgust the first time I rode " Copper-Nob." The Levis team used to start from Ballacraine in those days, and we set off together, he on a " 250 " and I on the " 175." He tried hard to lose me all the way to Ramsey, but I held him and though he did not know it, held him on about half throttle!

When we had rounded the Hairpin I opened up and left him standing. I finished the lap to Ballacraine—my first lap on " Copper-Nob "—in a time equal to the fastest practice lap of any " 175 " to date, and except for a mile or so past

Ramsey Hairpin, when I was "showing" old Phil, I had never used full throttle. When I did try, the next day, I lapped easily, from Ballacraine, in 43 minutes, some two minutes faster than any of the "175" four-strokes. My "Douglas to Douglas" laps, officially timed by the A-C.U., were always slow, for they included a four or five minutes stop at Ballacraine. We had worked the "book" properly and when I started the odds were 20 to 1 against me. But that race was in the bag.

I had my plans laid, too, for after the race. After I had won I was going to ask the Butterfields to take me into the Levis firm. I had already won a T.T. and several Grands Prix for them, and I figured that a second T.T. on "Copper-Nob," with the possibility of a couple more Continental Grands Prix to follow, would give me a name and reputation which would justify me a position on the Board of Directors. Furthermore, I had views on sales and publicity and, as a motorcycling journalist, on that vital thing "What the public wants," which, I think, would have been invaluable to a small family concern which was composed of engineers rather than business men and salesmen. I had mentioned the idea tentatively to Bill Butterfield and he had said neither "yes" nor "no." I felt that the Ultra-Lightweight pot would turn the scale. I had just got to win the "175" race, and my business future was assured. Nothing seemed easier.

There was a mass start in that 1924 Ultra-Lightweight, the first time that such a thing occurred in the history of the T.T. races. There were 17 of us in all, and by virtue of having won the 1922 Lightweight I had an early number.

The maroon fired, and we were off like a flash. My Levis started with two hefty foot-slogs—I was sitting astride it—and I was flat on the tank in a few seconds and away towards Bray Hill alone. Anxious punters, who fancied I was a dark horse, saw me flash past St. Ninians a hundred yards ahead of the field, and rushed to the bookies to put their shirts on me before the positions were recorded at Ballacraine! I took

Bray Hill flat out and at the bottom looked over my shoulder. A straggling stream of also-rans was on the crest of the hill. The race was in the bag . . .

And then things started to happen. At Braddan the motor began to pink, and by Union Mills Wal Handley, Jock Porter and one or two others had passed me. Leaden-hearted, I plodded on with ever-lessening speed and that " heavy " feel in the engine that tells of pre-ignition. And so it was; I had a non-stop run, but finished a bad fourth. That was that.

Glumly, Bob Newey attributed the trouble to the fact that the cooling system, although satisfactory enough in the cool of early morning practising, was inadequate for the midday heat. " There's no time to do anything before the French Grand Prix," he said. " You'll have to take it easy and hope Wal Handley isn't there." Wal wasn't there, but a couple of Frenchmen (height of humiliation!) set the pace and I finished third.

I was utterly depressed by this time, but when I returned to the works Bob met me with a smile. " I know what's been the trouble, Dave—I can put it right in two minutes. I promise you that you'll win the Belgian. If only I'd realized it before, it might have been different . . . "

With a few dabs of a brush he covered those burnished copper radiating flanges with cylinder black . . . The Affair of the Black Paint.

It did make all the difference. What we had not realized was that burnished copper, though a fine conductor of heat, is a very poor transmitter of it, but that blackened it is as good a transmitter as conductor. We proved it by putting two exactly similar pieces of copper, one burnished and one black, in an oven and bringing them to the same temperature. Then we removed them and hung them up to cool. The burnished one stayed hot for an hour, but the black one was stone cold in 10 minutes; it was transmitting its heat, while the burnished one was retaining it, just as it had retained it in " Copper-Nob."

With a dull black cylinder I went to Belgium and won the
" 175 " class by nearly half an hour, also finishing third in
the " 250." But it was too late; the T.T., the only race that
counted, had been lost.

So I became a journalist instead of a manufacturer, and
the Levis firm continued in a small way to make a small number of very excellent motorcycles. A few dabs of black paint
—and it might have been different . .

TRAILER TACTICS

By Tyrell Smith.

In the late twenties it was the custom of those British riders
who took part in the principal Continental races to travel
around by train. This was expensive, sometimes slow, and
often resulted in the temporary loss of the dicing machinery,
In this latter connection, I well remember a train trip from
Rotterdam to Leipzig. On the frontier of Luxembourg, at a
tiny station called Trois Vièrges, just as the train moved off,
I was rewarded with the pleasing sight of my bicycle and
precious box of tools being wheeled along the opposite plat-
form rapidly back in the direction of Holland! After three
days of hectic telephoning, everything eventually arrived
safely in Leipzig.

It was incidents such as these that made British riders consider other forms of transport, and I believe it was in 1931
that the first British-manned car and trailer took part in the
Circus, driven by Syd and Les Crabtree. On their arrival at
the Stations Koffiehuis, Assen, for the Dutch T.T., Les re-
counted that on leaving the Customs at the Belgian-Dutch
frontier Syd took the wheel. He remarked shortly afterwards
how well the device, a small Standard, was going, and con-
cluded that it must be due to the Dutch petrol. An hour or
more later, pulling up by the roadside, they discovered the
trailer was missing! Hastily retracing their steps, they found
the trailer not many miles from the frontier, right side up, and
with everything intact.

My own first attack on the Continent with a trailer was in 1933, in company with Charlie Manders and three Rudges. The motive power was a Talbot " 75 " which had already covered 50,000 miles, and the trailer was a rather rough and ready affair, very reminiscent of an open cattle truck. At this time we knew nothing of the subtleties of weight distribution applied to a trailer, and perhaps it was as well we didn't.

Before taking the Talbot to the Isle of Man, the brakes had been giving a bit of trouble, and, time being very precious, I had them " attended to " by a garage in Coventry. This " attention " proved so satisfactory that shortly after arriving in the Island, one of the front brake cross-shafts seized solid and put the foot brake completely out of operation. Time was so short, and what there was was invariably spent on the bicycles, that I didn't get a chance to rectify the brakes until we arrived in Berlin, having travelled from Liverpool to Coventry, Coventry to Harwich, the Hook of Holland to Assen, Assen to Berne and Berne to Berlin, a total of about 1700 miles! We never hit a thing, largely due to the fact that the Talbot had some real rear wheel brakes, operated by a lever reminiscent of a railway signal box! But more so, I think, to our ignorance of the habits of trailers. We had things so arranged that the trailer was almost in balance about its own axle. This led, as we soon found out, to colossal side-sway, which automatically limited our maximum speed to about 40 m.p.h. To attempt to drive any faster was too nerve-racking to be sustained—consequently we had to travel at a reasonably safe speed.

This trailer had standard Morris pressed steel wheels, which quickly objected to the stresses caused by the side-sway, and split at the welds. We bound them with wire, we arranged for spares in advance, we welded them up again in the most odd little Continental villages, and actually kept going until we reached Dunchurch, ten miles from Coventry, on the return journey.

This trip was crammed with incident, made all the more novel by virtue of its being our first trip by trailer. To mention but one: after the Dutch race, in which I was a non-starter due to an attack of tonsilitis, I stayed on in Rotterdam to recover, and finally flew to Berne. The outfit afterwards proceeded to Berne in the hands of Charlie Manders, Matt McQuaid and Bert Baguley. Limping into Cologne, with nasty noises coming from the gearbox, they were providentially put in touch with Jack Woodhouse. Not only did Jack have a replacement ball race of the correct pattern, but he had a fitter who had served his time with Clement-Talbot Ltd. and knew the car from stem to stern! They were on their way rejoicing within twenty-four hours, having had a night's sleep as well.

I did the Continental trip alone in 1934, so went by rail, but the following year we laid our plans early, and I traded in the Talbot, by this time decidedly the worse for wear, having covered 96,000 miles, for a new 27 h.p. Vauxhall. Charlie Manders built a really super trailer, complete with almost dust-proof cover, and definitely heavy on the front this time. This trailer followed so well, as we subsequently found, that under favourable conditions 85-90 m.p.h. could be maintained with perfect safety.

Our first trip with this outfit was planned to start from Coventry, after the 1935 T.T., the crew consisting of Charlie Manders and Alan Bruce with a couple of Excelsiors, and myself with a 250 Rudge. We had arranged to rendezvous at about 6 p.m. at the Plough Hotel, the home of that very worthy sportsman, Ned Potter, and prior to this rendezvous the bicycles had never been loaded into the trailer. After a very convivial evening, we parked ourselves around the corner, under a street lamp, and proceeded to load up. This necessitated quite a lot of trial and error, and nailing and screwing blocks to the floor of the trailer to locate the wheels of the bicycles. The job took about four hours, and we eventually went on our way rejoicing, and I should think greatly to the relief of the residents of Croft Road, at about 2 a.m.

This outfit proved extremely reliable and I recollect no incidents connected with it until Charlie Manders and I were on the way to Berne in April, 1936. We were pushing it along the pavé of the French Route National as hard as we could, to get to Berne before midnight, when Chas. remarked that the steering appeared a bit light. I said it was only his imagination, and on we went. Some time later he said it was getting worse, and a glance back at the trailer revealed that all was definitely not well. Our tow-bar was attached to the bumper brackets, and we found that one bracket had broken at its point of attachment to the chassis, leaving that end of the bar in mid-air. All we could rustle up to do a temporary repair was some strong iron wire, with which we bound things together, and more by luck than anything else we got to Berne without the other bracket breaking.

I had a most epic trip from Tyseley to Liverpool, on the way to the Isle of Man in 1936. We had worked day and night to get the four-valve O.H.C. 249 Excelsiors ready, and I was all set to leave the Works with the first complete bicycle at ten minutes past one, to catch the 3 o'clock boat! Before I left the Works, Mr. Walker 'phoned the I.O.M. Steam Packet Company to ask them to hold the boat, so I knew I had a sporting chance. Round about Ivetsey Bank, a glance in the mirror showed me that the lashings securing the bicycle were coming loose, and it was almost on its side. I didn't dare risk the possibility of damage, so had to pull up and re-lash it, losing about seven precious minutes.

The Old Vauxhall fairly whistled along, and on a nice stretch of concrete road near Bromborough I was well in the eighties. I noticed an empty Ford Eight parked by the road-side, and just after passing it was prompted to look in the mirror. Two very large policemen fairly shot out of the ditch and made such a rush at the little Ford that I'm sure they got jammed in the doors. Anyway, I kept motoring, and

never saw the Ford again. Much to my surprise, I was not
stopped at the entrance to the Tunnel, and I made the landing stage at twenty past three, with the I.O.M. boat fairly
panting to be off as soon as the Excelsior and I were hauled
aboard. The car and trailer were left on the quayside, but a
telegram to the A.A. soon had them fixed up safely.

This Vauxhall and the Manders trailer took us in safety
and without incident around the full Continental Circus in
'36 and '37 and on a somewhat abbreviated tour in '38.
These trips were tremendously interesting and full of fun.
I can most thoroughly recommend travel by trailer instead of
by train, provided one does not object to long hours and hard
work. But it is worth it all, and leaves one with enough
pleasant memories to last a lifetime.

THE CRIME IN THE FARMYARD
BY HAROLD ROWELL.

In the 1937 M.G.P. a gentleman appeared of the name of
Knowles, whose profession was given in the Programme as
" Chicken Sexer."

Knowles, like most of us, was not altogether swamped with
this world's goods, and the 250 (home-hatched) Rudge which
he was riding was a far from new-laid affair, and had developed into a rather ugly duckling.

By the end of the practice week, with only Monday morning left to qualify, Knowles had done all his practice laps
except the timed one, which had to be completed in 75 minutes—I believe that was the time for a 250 in those days.

The Rudge mechanic, the late Mr. Wills, cornered me and
suggested that as in his opinion (it was mine, too) it is the
" little man " who makes the sport, he felt it would do me
no harm to follow Knowles on that Monday morning with a
bag of spanners and spares and see to it that he got his
" fast lap " in.

We set off in good style, but at the top of Creg Willys hill,
just as you come on to the straight, his engine seized—apparently this was its usual seizing point!

As this was his last chance, and as he remarked almost tearfully to me that his ambition in life was a starter's badge, I suggested that we remove both machines into the nearby farmyard for adjustments.

Here we set to and changed the numbers, so that he proceeded on my practice machine (also a 250 Rudge) and I was left to try and unseize his. His parting remark before he sped off to achieve his ambition was that he would be grateful if I could get his machine back to Douglas early enough to have it ready for weighing in that afternoon. This seemed easy enough until I found the ――― thing wouldn't start!

Well, I coasted and pushed—mostly pushed—all the way to Kirkmichael, arriving there just in time to catch the first train to Douglas—and believe me, I was ready for a sit-down!

Being young and having a healthy respect for the Chief Marshal (which has increased with the years) I then lived in a blue funk lest news of my terrible crime should leak out, and I should be on the carpet and Knowles would be excluded. I didn't feel quite right until I met Knowles after presentation night, wearing his coveted starter's badge. It didn't worry him that he hadn't finished: he had started, and that was what mattered to him!

THEY HAD ME ON A FORK
By Wilmot Evans.

My most vivid recollection is of the 1926 T.T. practising. The late Harold Willis was riding for the same marque as I was on, and he proclaimed loudly that the plot didn't steer. After heated arguments with the No. 8 hats, it was decided that in all secrecy a pair of proprietary forks should be fitted to my machine for the next morning's practice, and this was done, unknown to me.

When I was waiting my turn to start that morning, the manager gave me instructions to come down Bray Hill at the end of my first lap at my limit, as all the Works No. 8 hats would be there to watch the steering. All round the first lap

I was deciding that this was the chance to prove the steering was poor, and in due course down Bray I went, in control and then out—all over the road—making a perfect two-point landing at the bottom and disappearing in a series of violent wobbles.

After breakfast I was summoned to The Mat. '' What,'' they asked, '' did I think I was doing on Bray? Trying to wreck the model?'' I replied, of course, '' We all told you it wouldn't steer!''—and then the awful truth came out: '' But the new forks you asked for were actually on your machine . . . ''

The last laugh was mine, however. When the times were given, my second lap was my fastest of the week!

MY FIRST CRACK AT BRAY HILL
By Chris. Tattersall.

I can recall several hectic moments in the Isle of Man, but my worst experience, I think, was in my first T.T. practice. All my pals(?) had said that unless one could take Bray Hill flat out, one might as well chuck the idea of being a T.T. rider, so I cracked off my first lap at a great rate.

I noticed that the machine seemed hard to hold on the road at places like Hilberry and so on, but I thought this was due to my lack of road racing experience. I came out of Governor's Bridge, wound the plot up along the Grandstand straight and was really cracking the whip as I went down Bray Hill. The machine took up all the road, and seemed to want the footpath, too—all I could see of the road was a grey blur. How I got to Quarter Bridge I don't know, but once there I had to go out wide (out of the corner of my eye I saw a Marshal move very quickly!) along to Braddan Bridge.

I hit the base of the war memorial coming out of the second Braddan bend, nearly went into the Post Office at Union Mills and a bit further along I decided that either I was no use, or there was something wrong. There was! Actually the rear tyre had gone almost completely flat towards the end of the first lap, and I also found that there wasn't a well-filler fitted . . . You can guess what I thought then, especially as the inner tube had pretty well disappeared, too.

No, I shall never forget that first practice morning!

FORGETTING AND REMEMBERING
By " Mavro."

It always seems rather extraordinary to me, the way in which one forgets incidents which, at the time of their occurrence, would certainly not be classed as trivial or uninteresting. The other day I met a fellow who said he had watched me hit the bolsters at Creg-ny-Baa during the 1926 Amateur T.T. I began hotly to deny this blot on my escutcheon—until, out of the mists of the past, came the picture of myself hurling that large, experimental 3-speed Scott into those bolsters, bouncing off somehow and hectically wobbling down the left-hand gutter.

Incidentally, about half-way through that race the engine seized solid along the Sulby Straight. I free-wheeled to the Bridge, pushed the bike into a field, and told the Marshal I was " R ". After about five minutes I went and had a look at the Scott: to my amazement, the engine was free. So I " un-retired " myself and carried on, to finish seventh! Those were the days!

In the following year, 1927, I had an amazing crash, of which I shall never need any reminder. Funnily enough, nobody saw it! For that year I had gone back to my old love, the two-speed Scott, and Shipley had built for me a wonderful little bike, more or less an exact replica of the 1925 Senior T.T. Scott. It developed 26 b.h.p. and weighed little more than 230 lbs. It was much too fast for the cycle parts—and for the owner!

On almost the last day of practice, I had just breasted the rise after Bray Hill, flat out and " howling " well, when it happened. There was no warning whatever and the first inkling I had that everything was not going to plan was when I found myself somersaulting through the air. Then I rolled

—how I rolled!—along the road, which is slightly downhill at this point, with the bike and the accompanying fireworks display careering along just behind. The strange " noises off " were heard at Quarter Bridge, and assistance soon arrived. Luckily neither my beloved two-speeder nor myself was much bent. But we were not allowed to start in the race.

The only reason for the crash that I could think of was a sudden engine seizure. A week or two later, when I was back home, I received a somewhat indignant letter from Harry Langman, informing me that there was no sign of a seizure and could I please explain why I had fallen off! I racked my brains, and then remembered noticing at the Start on that fateful morning that the bracket securing the front mudguard to the fork crown was cracked. I asked Harry to examine the front mudguard; and the mystery was then explained without doubt. The guard had touched the tyre and gone round with the wheel, causing the machine to somersault at over 80 m.p.h.

DILEMMA IN THE DUTCH
By Artie Bell.

The event was the 1947 Dutch Senior T.T. The other races, including the Junior, were held the same day and there had been a series of delays for one reason or another. Each race was 15 to 20 minutes late starting and consequently when Harold Daniell and I prepared to warm up the big Nortons for the Senior I thought I should have time for a final look-see at a particularly nasty little hairpin bend just beyond the start.

The heat that day, by the way, was terrific, the hottest recorded in Holland for 112 years, and you can easily guess the state the tarred roads were in. However, I rode slowly down to the hairpin, had a look, and turned to come back. This seemed to be the signal for all the officials in sight to pounce on me. They held tight on to the bike and did a lot of talking, while I tried to explain matters in my best Dutch which consists of three words, none of which could be worked into the argument.

Anyway, it transpired that I could not go back to the start except by doing a complete lap, and of course I had a soft plug in the bike, and no crash hat, gloves and so forth. Off I went as quickly as I thought the soft plug would allow, and arrived back at the start to find this was the one race they intended to start on time, as it was being broadcast!

I was met by " The Professor " (Joe Craig), quite un-flurried though a trifle anxious, complete with racing plug, crash hat, etc., and just as Joe was getting the soft plug out of a very hot engine the race started—massed start, with myself and Joe in the front line!

All praise to " The Professor " : with the whole pack screaming round him he managed to change the plug while I got the hat on, etc. Incidentally, I inadverently let the machine sway to one side, and Joe's finger got badly burned, but I only learned of this afterwards, for he never let out a squeak at the time. It seemed an endless delay to me, but actually he managed to get me started only 20 seconds behind the pack, and it says a lot for the urge of the big Norton that I was able to come round at the end of lap 1 (eight or nine miles per lap) in seventh place. By lap 3 I was in third position, then second (Harold retired with a puncture) and on lap 5 or 6 I took the lead, which happy state of affairs lasted until the end of the race.

SMALL BEGINNINGS

By Les Archer.

The time, May, 1932. Preparations are in hand for the first visit to the Isle of Man.

Ten days before official practising is due to start, a 1931 K.T.T. is groomed for a road trip to Liverpool to catch the afternoon boat to the Isle of Man. Tools for the servicing of a racing machine are packed carefully in a haversack. A very limited gent's natty wardrobe is packed in another, and the rider in full leather racing kit takes off with a machine in the early hours of the morning.

On arrival in the Island, unheralded by any swarms of autograph hunters, or plaudits from old friends, the rider makes a quiet run up to Onchan, looking for " The Old Manx Arms." Duly installed, the great adventure is on. The plan is to do as many laps with the roads open as can be crammed into one week, an average of about nine a day.

Then comes the great day, to collect a grand new K.T.T., one of many that have just arrived, all wrapped up and bearing such labels as " Joe Sarkis," " Jimmy Lind," " Dave Brewster," etc., etc. Off come the brown paper and tank wrapping from the one labelled " L. J. Archer," in goes the petrol and oil; and then are heard the first notes of the engine that is to be called upon to propel the rider in his first T.T.

The official practice period passes safely and it is soon realised that, for a first year rider, the plot is to learn the course thoroughly to Ramsey and let the Mountain take a secondary place in the plan of campaign, bearing in mind that is it generally shrouded in mist, anyway.

A further resolution is made that caution is essential and this, coupled with particular care as to the mechanical side and acceptance of the advice of the late Harold Willis (" Learn how to ride it and don't try to tune it ") brings about the satisfactory result of sixth place. The first step on the T.T. ladder.

BAD TIMES AND GOOD TIMES
By David Whitworth.

Two painful occasions come first into my memory—the first involving mental pain and the second, physical.

In the 1939 Junior T.T. I rode six laps without a right-side footrest. That was distinctly uncomfortable, of course, but what was much worse than the discomfort was my conviction that my lost footrest had cost a life. It sounds incredible, but the thing had been wiped off my machine by

Waddington's head, as he was slowly crawling across the road after a tumble " round the corner " of Bray Hill. I had no chance to avoid him and was convinced I must have killed him—the rest of the ride was a nightmare from which I didn't recover until I found he was O.K.

My most uncomfortable ride apart from the above was a three-lap " outer " at Brooklands on my Rex Acme with the saddle over the back wheel. During the first lap a rear saddle-stay bolt broke, and got mixed up with the spokes of the back wheel. Several spokes broke at the hub, and flying out from the rim tried hard to puncture my sit-upon, which was projecting over the rear of the saddle! Did I stand on the footrests quickly? With well dropped handlebars I couldn't " get up," so I finished the race—and won it—standing on the footrests with my bottom higher than my head. The spokes had penetrated my leathers, and I had bruises for weeks!

Now for some happier memories. The most wonderful rides I have ever had were when I rode Stanley Wood's 500 Works Velocette in the 1938 Ulster and Donington Jubilee meeting. It was a wonderful machine and at Donington I had a real battle with one of the finest sportsmen I ever expect to meet—Ginger Wood, riding its sister machine. I shall never forget that ride: absolutely first-class, all of its 60 miles.

Another thing I shall always remember is the happy and informal atmosphere about most of the Brooklands meetings, when all the officials were old pals of the riders and everything was run with an air of " Here we all are, come down for another afternoon of sport with a picnic thrown in." It reminds me of the comradeship which you found in the frontline men of the Eighth Army in the Desert and Italy. The same kind of thing—at Brooklands it would be " Well, this is my last plug, old man, but if you're stuck you can have it," just as in the front line it was, " Well, this is my last half-mug of water, old boy, but if you've got a bit of shrapnel through your water-bottle, you can have half." Happy days!

THE HAT-TRICK THAT WASN'T
By Jock Porter.

I look on 1924 as my unucky T.T. year, for although I won the Ultra-Lightweight race, two spots of real bad luck just stopped me winning the Junior and the Lightweight— and I would have liked to make that hat-trick.

I went over for the practising, and on the Sunday, after only five days' practice, I was out touring with a friend, when unfortunately his machine ran into the rear of mine, with the result that I was laid up in bed until the day of the first race, i.e. the Junior.

I had had a broken rib and a punctured lung, and naturally I was feeling a bit weak, so I considered myself lucky to be ready in time for the Junior. On the third lap in this race I was lying third when my rear brake seized up. If that hadn't happened I might well have won, for the two riders in front of me both retired later.

On the Wednesday I had no difficulty in winning the Ultra-Lightweight. Then Friday came, and the Lightweight race. I had won this the previous year, and everything went well this time until the last lap. I was actually leading, comfortably, but I was given the wrong signal from my pit. This misled me into going all out on this final lap, and at Glen Helen I laid the machine over a little too far. The footrest touched the road and trailed me round, so that I struck the rock with the back wheel, which was badly buckled. Result —a crash and another near-win wiped out.

A FIRST LESSON
By Ted Pink.

My most vivid memory connected with the earlier days concerns a lesson which most riders learn sooner or later, and the sooner the better, provided that it ends the right way!

It was my first ride at Syston Park about 1928 on a "home-tuned" K.S.S. Velocette, in a 20 laps "do" The first part of the race proceeded reasonably well and the Course seemed to become a little easier—a dangerous period for a beginner. Ernie Thomas, on a "real" Velocette, came by up the straight, incidentally showering hard sharp stones behind him, and I thought it might be possible to hang on to his tail and learn a bit more about the Course—so I tried!

The next section ran slightly downhill, narrow and twisty, finishing up with a hump and a quick right and left and then through a gateway between a pair of iron gateposts. We approached the hump faster than I had previously tried, but I thought "If he can, I can," and hung on. I took the hump at about the same place as E.T. did, but unfortunately at a slightly different angle, and was not pointing in the right direction while aviating—the result was hectic and frightening. The bicycle, of course, took charge with a full-lock wobble and the back wheel hopping all over the road, in fact as a bicycle generally behaves when mishandled. However, I somehow managed to point it in the right direction to get through the gateway—a very frightened and surprised, but much less ambitious young "dicer."

The next few laps were employed in (a) getting the pulse back to normal and (b) trying to find out why Ernie could take that hump and winding bit safely whilst I could not. I learned a lot and found that by taking the previous bend differently and almost scraping the wall just before the hump, one could get through the section quite comfortably.

Moral! Just because another man can take a section fast, it does not necessarily mean that you can. Get the right line before trying the right speed.

At Greenford Dirt-track in the late twenties, we all fell off very often and in every conceivable way, my efforts in this direction being well up to average.

After one such fall and consequent head-first slide on my back, I picked myself up and felt a little peculiar. It seemed that I had painfully injured that part of me which should have been on the saddle! I was just beginning to get really worried when I discovered that sliding on my back had broken my braces and my breeches were filled up with the sharp clinkers and ashes which normally comprised the surface at Greenford. Fortunately, such falls usually caused a heavy dust cloud, and before it had cleared the breeches were emptied and re-adjusted—at least sufficiently to walk off the course!

ORDEAL BY FIRE

By Rem Fowler.

For a really hectic moment my recollection goes right back to the first T.T., in 1907. About halfway through the race, as I approached the Devil's Elbow (on the old course) between Kirkmichael and Peel, I saw clouds of black smoke on the hill ahead of me. As I rounded the bend, there in the middle of the road was a machine, well alight, with flaming oil and petrol all over the road.

I had to make up my mind instantly whether to obey the violent flag-wagging of the Boy Scout on duty, and stop, or to take a chance and dash through it. Realizing that I had a good chance of winning, I decided to make a dash for it. The Boy Scout and others standing by were naturally taken by surprise, and only just got out of the way in time as I vanished into the flames. The chief risk actually was of hitting the burning machine, which was hidden in flames and smoke. However, I managed to dodge it, and got through O.K.—all I felt was the hot blast. But I was very pleased to be on my way again, none the worse for what might have been a very nasty mess-up. And incidentally, of course, I won the race —" through the flames to victory," you might say.

I had plenty of other incidents, both amusing and thrilling, in the six T.T.'s I competed in, but this one stands out in my memory most clearly.

DRINKING HUMBLE PIE

By Geoff Davison.

I walked into the Falcon Cliff bar one night and ordered a whisky and soda. I was dressed in an almost new sports jacket, made by Birmingham's Best Tailor (price £15 15s. od. and 13 coupons), a beautiful Fair Isle Pullover (price £6 19s. 6d. and 6 coupons) and a natty pair of pre-war flannel bags (price 11s. 9d. and 5% discount for cash). I had come straight from the T.T. Special office and was pretty dirty.

The chap behind the bar looked at me. (He couldn't see my trousers, anyway). " We've got a drop of whisky," he said, " but it's a bit expensive for the likes of you."

I thanked him for his warning and went into the smoke-room, where Jock West bought me one. Which only goes to show . . .

DOG-GED DOES IT

By C. S. Barrow.

I can think of many hectic incidents, but the one that stands out most vividly in my memory is the story of the dog in the later stages of the 1928 Lightweight race.

During the last three laps of the race I was engaged in a struggle with Eddie Twemlow for second position. First he would lead for a few seconds, then I would get a slight advantage, and so it went on. On the last lap I was approaching Ramsey Square, having left braking to a very late point (trying to save every second) when the dog rushed out from the crowd.

The spectators, in all good faith, tried to drive the dog away, but this of course had the opposite effect—it rushed from one side of the road to the other, so that dog and machine were dodging each other until the correct line for the corner was completely lost and a crash seemed certain. Fortunately, however, this disaster was avoided; I completed the course without further trouble and was lucky enough to finish in second place.

KILLED 1917 — STILL GOING STRONG
By Howard Davies.

It was Mark Twain, I believe, who described the premature reports of his own death as " grossly exaggerated." It is not an unique experience to read one's own obituary, but it is certainly an uncanny one, and it remains for me the most remarkable recollection of my career as a rider.

My regretted demise occurred during the 1914-18 war. Turning up old files of " Motor Cycling," I find a paragraph headed " Well-known Motorcyclist in the R F.C. Killed in Action." It is illustrated with a photograph of " the late Lieut. Davies after finishing second on a $3\frac{1}{2}$ h.p. Sunbeam in the 1914 T.T." " Amateur and professional motor cyclists alike," it reads, " will remember the intrepid airman as a very successful competition rider, and winner of a number of medals and cups . . . We feel assured that all motor cyclists who knew him in the old days will share with us keen regret for the loss of this promising rider," and it gives in brief outline the details of my riding career and military service with the Royal Engineers and the Royal Flying Corps. Its comment is kindly flattering, but its facts are all correct except the central one: I was not dead! I might say, however, that on reading that notice I was tickled to death at being alive . . .

LIGHTER MOMENTS
By Chris. Tattersall.

Here is a bunch of comic little memories picked at random, some connected with the T.T. and others with other occasions:—

The impromptu mannequin parades we used to stage at the old Falcon Cliff Hotel, when the girls very kindly lent us filmy nightdresses, etc. I can still remember Paddy Johnston standing silhouetted against the light in a very insubstantial drapery, posing as a film star and not realizing how profiles are revealed in such settings.

A crowd of us very seriously offering our tobacco pouches round amongst friends. The contents, if they would burn at

all, tasted lousy—being composed of shredded brake linings . . .

Being dared—and accepting the challenge—to slide a large
ice-cream down the back of a feminine member of our party.

Eating a five or six course meal at Collinson's restaurant,
the courses being composed alternately of large ices and chips
—I reckon we must have been daft that time!

Presenting a " doctored " crash hat for checking. It was
a very old one and the top was broken in, but this had been
neatly covered with paper and carefully painted to match.
The bloke in charge, however, was very thorough about
examining helmets and he pressed his thumb on the top: the
look on his face when it went clean through was a tonic! Goes
to show, however, that you can't pull a fast one on them
where crash-hats are concerned and get away with it; all to
the good, no doubt.

Getting mistaken for Jock West. Neither us of thinks we
are a bit like the other, but this has happened so often that
we have come to an arrangement to sign each others auto-
graphs as and when required.

Then there was the 100-mile race at Southport on a very
hot day, so hot that just leathers over your birthday suit was
all you could bear to wear. Sand has a well-known retarding effect, and when I came to get off the model I slid forward—but my pants stayed where they were . . . when I
stood up they were hanging round my feet. Talk about
being caught with your pants down! Being a bit dazed, I
just stood there, while my mechanic seemed much more
worried about the bike than about me. Why did the crowd
laugh?

And that reminds me, to finish with, of an occasion in the
early days of dirt-tracking, when I got involved in a nasty
pile-up and was knocked right out. When I came round, it
was to find I had been completely stripped down and several
young nurses were gravely examining the extent of the
damage. I was very young then . . .

FORTY YEARS ON

By Geoff Davison.

[*This article was written in the autumn of 1942, and is reproduced by courtesy of " Motor Cycling " in which paper it appeared in serial form*]

> Forty years on, growing older and older,
> Shorter in wind, as in memory long . . . .
>
> Harrow School Song

FORTY years of motorcycling! That makes one think, But, actually, I am not so old after all, for I started very young.

Yes, I started young, during the summer holidays following my eighth birthday. Needless to say, I was not " in charge " of the various museum pieces which whirled me, at great risk but in a delirium of delight, through the streets and suburbs of Birmingham, home of motorcycles. Frequently these contraptions cast me from them and I would limp home, bruised and bleeding, with the thin story that " Rugger had been rather rough." It has never ceased to amaze me that my father, who, besides being a very wise man, was a master at my own school, did not pursue these " Rugger injuries " with my house master. Perhaps he did —and let the matter drop; for he was a very wise man!

It was in 1902 that I had my first ride, perched in a basket affair attached to the front of a De Dion tricar, as a sort of human battering ram. Fortunately, on the occasions when I was used as such, the blows were of a glancing nature, and I survived until the age of 12. My friend then replaced this lethal weapon by a Minerva motorcycle, and I assumed a somewhat precarious perch on the carrier.

The Minerva was, of course, a single-geared, belt-drive, tank-control job, and its use involved dangers of a different kind. It used to skid frequently and heartily, and though I soon mastered the art of mounting on the move, I often came a box of tacks when dismounting at speed half way up a hill on which it was about to conk.

My friend was always furious if he failed on a climb and had to return (less me) to the bottom, and after such an occurrence would not offer me another ride for weeks. My job was to hop it at the critical moment—and I became very skilled at judging that moment. If I left it too late—conk!—and no more rides for a time. If I slid off too early, I naturally could not run fast enough to keep on my feet — hence those nasty " Rugger knees." Judging it to a nicety was difficult, but I learnt the trick in time. People say " The lessons learnt in childhood are the most valuable." I agree. The lessons I learnt on that Minerva taught me instinctively to realize just whether a machine would conk or climb, and that knowledge contributed to some successes I have had on single-geared motorcycles.

Then my friend went and got married and the Minerva era ended. It was a dreadful blow at the time—how I hated the woman; but by then I was 14 and old enough (in those days) to be the legal rider of a motorcycle. That was grand; the trouble was getting the motorcycle, or rather, the money to buy it.

My father was dead against motorcycles; I had no wealthy relatives to touch. I was due for another two years at school, and, even after school, had no immediate prospects of earning money. But a motorbike I must have. So I started to raise the wind.

First I broke up my stamp collection, which was a fair one, for my father, in addition to being a schoolmaster, was a scientist with a large overseas " mailing list." I mounted the stamps on " Approval Sheets," advertised them in the " Boys' Own Paper " and sold quite a lot. Then, one Easter holiday, I started selling books—my school prizes went first; but I followed them up with the usual Christmas present books that every boy accumulates.

I began to learn the book trade and found a pawnbroker who sold me Henty's books at 6d. a time, which I resold to a second-hand bookseller at a bob or " one and a kick," according to condition. Unfortunately, this seam ran dry, and I was forced into dealing in a market with which I was unfamiliar. I vividly remember chancing 1s. 3d. on an early

edition of the Prayer Book in five volumes. My friendly
bookseller regarded them sorrowfully and offered me twopence the lot—a shattering blow.

I hawked them round every bookseller's in Birmingham for
days without an offer, and, finally, in despair, tried them on
an antique dealer. (Certainly they looked old enough to be
in his line!) He looked at me suspiciously and then, business
instinct overcoming his scruples, said, " They're not worth
much—say five bob." I staggered from his shop in a daze—
no Prayer Books before or since have brought me so near to
heaven—and I was only slightly set back when I saw them in
the window next day marked " Unique Edition—only £5."
Well, I had made 300 per cent. profit and I had enough Scots
blood in me to be satisfied with that.

Things were now looking brighter. I had raised £4 during
those Easter holidays, and I studied the small ads. in
" Motor Cycling " more keenly than ever. Machines boast-
ing magneto ignition, handlebar control, or M.O.I.V.
(mechanically operated inlet valve) were, of course, beyond
me, but it seemed that, for a fiver, I could pick up something
with, at least, a spray carburettor. How dreadful was my
disappointment when I cycled myself out to examine a few
such models. They would have needed an engineer to make
them go, and I was a schoolboy of 15.

Eventually, I decided that the only thing to do was to buy
the bits and build a machine. And, having reached that decision, " Motor Cycling " small ads. came up to scratch. A
firm in London was selling off some 1⅓ h.p. Clement-Garrard
engines, several years old but unused, for £3 apiece. Three
quarters of my savings went off by post that night, and in due
course the little Clement engine, carefully packed and
obviously quite new, arrived at my home to my unutterable
joy and my parents' profound disgust. I felt I was a motorcyclist—I had an engine, anyway.

The erection of " my darling Clementine " took over a year
to complete, owing largely to lack of capital. I picked up a

bit here and a bit there, as cash permitted. I even raised a pair of spring forks and a B. and B. handlebar-controlled carburettor. The final thing I wanted was a front wheel, but as apart from that " Clementine " was ready for the road, I used the front wheel of my push-bike! It was a 28-in. wheel and the back one was a 26-in., but it made no difference to the performance.

The specification of my first love was, roughly, as follows: Engine: Clement-Garrard, 56 by 63 mm., 156 c.c. (I think), overhead valves with automatic inlet; floating gudgeon pin secured by piston ring; detachable cylinder head; outside fly-wheel.

Ignition: Battery and coil, with plug on near side of cylinder, immediately opposite a quickly removable compression plug.

Carburetter: B. and B. h.b.c.

Frame: Bicycle.

Transmission: Belt, twisted leather—gear ratio 6 to 1.

Spring Forks: Druid.

Saddle: Brooks, bicycle type.

Tyres: 26 by 2-in. back, 28 by 1¾-in. front.

Footrests: One cricket stump, through bottom bracket of frame.

Lighting Set: One " Demon " cycle oil lamp (cost, new, 10½d.).

Valve Lifter: None.

Brakes: None.

Speed: 28 m.p.h.

Climbing Abilities: About 1 in 15.

As there were no brakes and no valve lifter, and, of course, no clutch or gear levers, or switches—I switched on by connecting the positive lead direct to the 6-volt Helleson dry cell which was tied on the back mudguard—the handlebars were definitely of the modern " clean " type. And by the way, apart from the fact that it had an automatic inlet valve, the engine was years ahead of its time, as its specification shows. Overhead valves, indeed, on an engine of 1903 vintage!

Question: Why were there no brakes?

Answer: Because I could not afford such luxuries. The engine had an outside fly-wheel, you will have noted, and a foot applied carefully to the flywheel rim had a marked retarding effect! I say "applied carefully" with intent; sudden application of the foot stopped the engine with the result that the twisted leather belt at once broke. The machine then raced on unimpeded, leaving the belt in the road, and the sequel was usually difficult. This always happened going down-hill—there was no need to apply the fly-wheel brake going up-hill; closing the throttle was effective enough!

The most "difficult" sequel I had was when the belt broke at the top of Birmingham Bull Ring—a tram-infested descent averaging about 1 in 12 for half a mile. I scampered down the wet wood-block surface in a series of hectic skids, entirely out of control. "Clementine" was no respecter of persons; she and I scattered pedestrians, parsons and policemen in our mad brakeless rush down Digbeth into Deritend. What the policemen would have said if they could have stopped me (and I would have welcomed being stopped by anything softer than a tram) or taken my number, I hardly like to think.

But as the front number plate was battered beyond recognition by countless crashes, and the back one was illegible as usual, I heard no more about the matter. The only damage done was a broken footrest in the final Deritend skid, and as I still had four of the set of six stumps left, that was a small matter. I returned home, after fitting another belt, by a different route (the machine wouldn't climb the Bull Ring anyway), a wiser, but not sadder, boy.

Many and varied were the experiences I had with "Clementine," and great was the knowledge I acquired. Ignition difficulties, of course, were paramount. The one failing of that engine was that the contact breaker was mounted on, and operated by, an extension of the exhaust valve cam. The slightest overdose of oil in the engine at once found its way on to contact breaker points—result, no spark. I suppose that, on the average, I stopped to clean oil off the contact breaker once in every 10 miles—certainly not more than 10, and probably less.

A good feature was that it was quite easy to see the spark —you just removed the compression tap (which, as I have said, was opposite the plug), applied your eye to the hole. and jiggled the contact breaker blade. If there was a spark. you could see it. A bad feature was that the spark usually ignited the residue of petrol vapour in the cylinder, so that a tongue of flame shot out and caught you in the eye. I remember stopping once at a wayside garage where the mechanic who served me looked at my machine sourly and said, " Ho! Clement-Garrard. Burnt your eyebrows yet?"

Later I fitted a magneto (again bought through the small ads. of " Motor Cycling "). This improved things, and I frequently did as much as 15 to 20 miles non-stop. But, owing to insecure fixing arrangements, the magneto used to flap about somewhat and the chain frequently flew off. (I could re-time that mag. and be off again in about 30 secs.). This gave me my first insight into pre-ignition, or perhaps I should say auto-ignition. I was scampering along one day, flat out as usual, when I happened to look down at the engine, only to see that the magneto chain had disappeared. Yet the engine was running perfectly! I had several spare chains in my pockets, of course, so I just carried on and did 10 miles more before I had to slow down for a big town, after which the plug cooled down and the engine decided that it needed a spark again.

Fuel was another problem. I forget now what petrol cost in those days, but it was far more than I could afford. On the other hand, my parents had a good supply of paraffin, and, even if I had to buy it, paraffin was cheaper than petrol. So I ran almost exclusively on paraffin.

My general procedure was to carry a medicine bottle of petrol in my pocket. I had fitted a small drain tap in the bottom of the float chamber; to start from cold I drained the paraffin from the carburettor, removed the float chamber top and filled it with petrol. At the critical moment when the float chamber had run nearly dry, I turned on the paraffin and all was well—usually, that is!

Once or twice I ran out of petrol, or lost my bottle. Starting then presented a problem, but necessity is the mother of invention. The first time this happened I removed my necktie, dipped it in the paraffin tank, wound it round the carburettor, and set fire to it. I then fanned the flames away from the tank, and when the carburettor had nearly reached melting point beat them out, turned on the paraffin and pushed off. The second and subsequent times I carried that tie as a spare " hot-spot "—it was no longer serviceable as a tie!

I rode " Clementine " for a year, at the end of which time she disintegrated when I was some 100 miles from home. Regretfully, I drained the paraffin from her tank and pushed her into the guard's van. The trouble was only a sheered exhaust cam spindle, which was easily repaired, but, for all she had taught me, she had broken my heart with her whimsical misdemeanours. Added to which I made the happy discovery that my father had reconciled himself to the fact that I was a confirmed motorcyclist.

One day he sadly inspected the machine. He had seen the set of cricket stumps dwindle to none and had noticed periodic family blitzes concerning the strange disappearance of the maid's broomsticks. He put two and two together, and gathered that I fell off a lot. When he realized that the machine had no brakes at all, he decided that a change of mount would be desirable and coughed up £10. I advertised "Clementine" in bits (still in "Motor Cycling's" small ads.), and sold them for nearly what they cost me to an unsuspecting

Irishman. With the proceeds I bought a 2½ h.p. 1911 Motosacoche for £16, and still had two quid to spare.

The Motosacoche was a disappointment. It was in apparently faultless condition, but it was gutless from the start, and nothing that I could do put any pep into it. I rode it for a year with much L.P.A. (" light pedalling assistance "), and finally it blew up, quite literally, in the middle of Birmingham, much to the indignation of passers-by who objected to being spattered with pieces of cylinder.

That explosion was the luckiest thing of my motorcycling life, for it brought me into contact with the Butterfield brothers, who were then beginning to make Levis motorcycles. (It was they who, eight years after, in 1921, gave me my first chance in the T.T.). It so happened that the explosion took place near the premises of the Birmingham Levis agents, and it was to their shop that I pushed the remains of the Motosacoche. Imagine my amazement when this firm offered me a brand-new Levis two-stroke for the pieces of Motosacoche and the trifling sum of £15. Dazzled by the prospect, I rushed off to raise the wind. It was easy— a friend who had been a frequent pillion passenger on the Motosacoche and was as sick of pushing it up hills as I was, had a secret hoard in Post Office Savings. He extracted it, and we went over to Stechford to collect the Levis.

What a thrill! Not only a shining new machine but actual contact with real manufacturers. The Butterfield brothers were in only a small way at the time, but they were turning out a highly efficient two-stroke and were selling them as fast as they could make them. I can find no fault whatever with that Levis, and, indeed, it was a machine well in advance of the time—1913. The 1919 and 1920 models were, I believe, different in detail only.

It was my first real motorcycle. " Clementine " had been neither powerful nor reliable; the Motosacoche was fairly reliable but entirely gutless; the Levis was immensely powerful (by comparison with the others) and dead reliable.

Except for an occasional broken belt I never had an involuntary stop.

I was now 18 and earning very small money as a chartered
accountant's articled clerk—a job I detested. But I had just
those few extra bob per week that made petrol possible, and
I never insulted the Levis's tank with paraffin. I became
trials minded, and Sunday after Sunday in the summer of
1913 a friend (also with a Levis) and I went hill-hunting in
Gloucestershire; Willersley, Saintbury, Sudeley, Rising Sun
were all visited. The first two we climbed fairly easily, but
Rising Sun, which was in an atrocious condition at the time,
defeated us utterly. Remember, we were on single-geared
211 c.c. machines.

But Sudeley presented possibilities Sunday after Sunday
we tried it, and each time we got a little nearer the top. My
pal and I soon realized that if we were to climb it we must
reduce weight and windage. Once we got that idea we were
well on the way to winning. By casting caps, coats, gloves
and tools, we got 20 yards higher up the hill! Finally, I
climbed it (my friend never did, to my intense gratification)
by removing all clothes except shirt, shorts and shoes, and
by detaching from the machine the carrier, toolbag, both
mudguards, stand, pump, lamps and, most important of all,
the silencer and plates. (The latter meant little in weight, but
they reduced silencer back pressure—and there were no
policemen about that day). In this racing trim I soared over
the top of Sudeley and felt that I had conquered the world.

More than ever I wanted to ride in a reliability trial, but
the Levis, grand machine as it was, was single geared, and
so quite useless against the three-speed chain-drive models
which were coming on to the market. In the autumn of 1913
the Sutton Coldfield club organized an open trial for the Levis
Cup, presented by the Butterfield brothers. I went and sold
myself to William Watson, father of Midland motorcycle sport
of the time and Birmingham Sunbeam agent. I must have
been a good salesman, for he agreed to loan me a " works "

2¾ h.p. Sunbeam. It was only a two-speeder, but, with a top gear of 7 to 1 and a bottom of 14, it was ideal for the job. An ideal machine for my first trial, and an open trial at that!

No, I didn't win it. Leslie Guy, on a Scott, did that. But out of over 100 competitors there were only ten gold medallists, and I was one of them. Was I proud! What did it matter that my employer, on inquiring into the reason for my absence from the office that Saturday morning, told me that I had no interest in my work and that I would never make a chartered accountant. I knew that better than he! What mainly interested me was that I had won a gold medal in my first trial; I little dreamt that the same Levis Cup would, 10 years later, become my own property as a result of winning it three years in succession—1921, '2 and '3—and on a Levis.

Towards the end of 1913 I decided that the Levis was not fast enough for me. I advertised it, again in "Motor Cycling," and exchanged it, no-cash-either-way, for a 3½ h.p. 1911 Rudge, No. "R906." If the owner of that Rudge is still reading "Motor Cycling," let me tell him that it was a fine machine. The power it had! Single-geared, that Rudge climbed the Nailsworth Ladder, with its gradient of, I believe, 1 in 2½. And it climbed the Old Wyche Cutting, with its maximum, at the top, of 1 in 2.9, with a pillion passenger.

The tyres were sadly bald—not too good for Cotswold mud in February—but the tyre firms were playing in those days. I wrote to a couple of them, told them that I was willing to use their tyres if they would supply me with a free pair, and what was their bonus for a cup, gold medal, etc.? To my intense surprise, each firm accepted me and sent me a pair of tyres! In a mistaken sense of decency I fitted one make on the front and the other on the back—and then broke a belt just before the lunch check. The "Colmore" in those days, and for some years afterwards, was a non-stop trial, and a stop of any sort put one out of it.

I was mad with disappointment, but I determined to put up a good show on Rising Sun, which came early in the afternoon. Being out of the trial, I stopped at the bottom to cool

down and pick my time, and then gave her the gun. I fairly
roared over the top, taking the final stretch, where dozens
were failing with wheelspin, at about 30 m.p.h. I got a good
" press," and the film taken of the hill showed that I was at
least twice as fast as anybody else.

Shortly after the 1914 " Colmore " I got a very bad dose
of influenza and was in bed for three weeks. As I began to
get better, the horror of going back to my unutterably dull job
bore down on me, and in a wild fit of hope I wrote to the
Editor of " Motor Cycling " and asked him to give me a job.

To my amazement he replied that there was a vacancy on
the staff, and would I let him know what I could do, and send
him some sample articles? Would I not! Propped up against
the pillows, I gave him of my best. Each time the post came
without a letter for me my hopes sank, and bitterness over-
whelmed me. But, finally, there was a letter, naming an
interview the following Monday.

I went through that interview in a daze, but I landed the
job, and the following Monday I was the junior member of
" M.C.'s " Editorial staff.

Those were grand days, and the next four or five months
were the happiest I had ever known. Then came the war.
On August 6, 1914, 36 hours after war had been declared, I
put my name down on a vast list at Putney barracks as a
Despatch Rider, and heard no more of it. After six weeks of
doubt and uncertainty, the telephone bell rang one day and
the officer commanding a new signal company which was just
forming asked if we could find him some D.Rs. Selby and I,
and one of " Motor Cycling's " artists, Singleton, joined on
the spot, and did not regret it. They were happy days, in the
ranks of that London Signal Company, and I learnt much
about traffic riding (still single geared) and motorcycle
maintenance, for, in spite of my youth, I got made " Cor-
poral Artificer."

During the last war I did a lot of riding, but it was
not the type of riding that I liked. Most of it, in fact,

on the shell-torn pavé roads of Flanders, I disliked intensely, although it certainly taught me how to handle a machine on rough stuff. Some few hundred miles I covered during occasional " leaves," but motorcycling as a sport was dead.

When the War-to-end-War ended, I became a motorcycle agent in Luton, Bedfordshire, and as soon as machines were available motorcycle sport re-opened full bore. The machines we rode were mostly five- or six-year-old renovated models, but there were a few ex-Army types and here and there a really new Douglas, P. and M. or Triumph—makes which had been in production for the Services throughout the war and so were early in the field with post-war products. But for the most part, motorcycle sportsmen were content with old crocks, newly painted.

One of the makes for which I was agent was the Levis and, believe me, I lost no time in renewing my acquaintance with the Butterfield brothers and Bob Newey, the works director. I not only sold many Levis machines—I managed to borrow a hot-stuff model for speed trials and hill-climbs, and won many medals on it. But as that particular Levis was loaned to many agent friends of the firm and was never beaten in two seasons' racing, I did not acquire exceptional prestige with it! I tried hard to get a Levis for the 1920 T.T. (first of the Lightweight classes), but although the Butterfields seemed to regard me favourably, they were not prepared to play. " Possibly next year," they said.

It was in the autumn of 1920 that I first had the chance to prove to the Butterfields (and to myself) that I could really handle a Levis pretty decently. That was in the first Levis trial, held for single-gear, belt-driven machines only. The Butterfields lent me a machine, nicely tuned for the job, and I came up from Luton the day before the trial to collect it. I knew nothing about the course, or the type of trial, except what had appeared in the rules and regulations, so several of the Levis Athletic Club lads had the advantage of me.

Still, it was my chance to show the Butterfields. There was nothing I could do in the way of tuning, no time for anything in the way of hill-learning. All I could do was to travel light —and my adventures six years before on the Cotswold Hills had taught me the value of that. I set off clothed as for a cross-country run.

Was it cold! At the lunch-stop I was so numbed that I had almost to be lifted from the machine. I gathered that I had done pretty well on the various hills, but my immediate ambition was something very strong in the way of spirits, and plenty of it. As chance would have it, I met an old war-time friend—and my ambition was realized. So much so, indeed, that after the lunch period I had almost to be lifted on to my machine; but fortunately this was not noticed.

One result of my elevated condition, however, was that I decided that my machine was not making nearly enough noise. I remembered the extra power obtained with silencer plates removed. At that time, police prosecutions for noisy motorcycles were at their zenith. " To hell with them," said Johnnie Walker and I. Off came the end plates, and up all the hills I roared! A comparative outsider, I beat the works cracks and won the trial in a canter.

The Butterfields thought well of that, although they did not know one reason for my " spirited " riding, and as a result promised me a mount for the 1921 Lightweight class of the Junior T.T. Before that came along, however, there was my old friend the " Colmore," in which the Levis Cup—premier award for my first Open Trial in 1913—was put up for best performance of a single-geared machine. In those days the Colmore was a pretty stiff trial for chain-driven three-speeders, so to attempt it on a single-geared " 250 " seemed the height of optimism; and, apart from the hills, this type of machine was most unsuitable, for the trial was non-stop throughout and one had to arrive at the various checks within one minute each way of schedule.

Still, a gang of single-gear enthusiasts essayed it. I was lucky, for by the lunch-stop I was the only " S.-G. " with clean sheet. In the afternoon I roared up Rising Sun almost as fast as I had on the Rudge in 1914—the power that " 250 two-stroke developed!—and was obviously well in the running for the cup. And then, 40 miles from home—40 miles of main roads—a back tyre puncture! Stop, mend it, and be out of the trial? No fear! I rode on flat, gradually losing time, but still in the running. Would the tyre (beaded-edge, of course) stay on the rim, would the back wheel remain intact, would my posterior stand the strain? For 30 miles the answer to all three was " yes "—so then I gave it the gun.

For the last 10 miles I was faced with averaging nearly 35 m.p.h. on a machine capable of only about 40—its one gear, with chain-cum-belt transmission, was $7\frac{1}{2}$ to 1—and the trip was more hectic than any I have had in many races. My progress was one long " snake "; often I cannoned from bank to bank; and corners were nightmares.

Further, the road was littered with gentlemanly competitors " losing time " before the final check. How they cursed me! But I did not actually hit any of them, or anything else though even now, over 20 years after, I vividly remember a dozen hair-raising escapes. At the finish, which I reached on time, I should have fallen from the machine had not some sportsman caught it and carried me from it. But I knew that I must have won the Levis cup and, sweeter even than that was a snatch of conversation I heard between Bill Butterfield and Alec Ross, when they both thought I was out for the count. " A damned good show—young Dave ought to do all right in the T.T." I had won the boss's praise and, bruised and hurt though I was, the world was mine.

And what a grand world it was! The thrill of the T.T.— how I counted the days and hours before I broke away from business and set off with a practice machine—one of the 1920 T.T. models—for the Isle of Man. The 1921 Coal Strike was

at its height and the I.O.M. Steam Packet Company was running reduced services. But we got there somehow on the old
" Fenella "—(not the fine ship of that name recently sunk by
enemy action)—after a very rough seven-hour crossing,
during which most of us were sick. But not I, oh no! I had
long before developed an anti-seasickness technique, which I
have always found infallible—recipe on application to the
Editor!

The Levis camp was at Peel, on the far side of the Island,
for, as Bill Butterfield sagely remarked, it was cheaper at
Peel than at Douglas, you could get more work done and you
were not persecuted by the " tradesmen." So my first ride
on Manx roads was from the quay at Douglas to Quarter
Bridge, along the course to Ballacraine and straight on to
Peel.

Oh, the glamour of those names—the magic of that road:
Kirk Braddan, Union Mills, Greeba, the Highlander. It was
indeed a different world from the straw hats of Luton, Beds.,
and the trivial hill-climbs and speed trials which had seemed
so important. Since the first T.T. in 1907 I had read every
word that " Motor Cycling " had published about the T.T.
races; now I was to ride in them myself and, furthermore,
was one of " Motor Cycling's " reporters for the practice
period. No wonder I was in a motorcyclist's heaven.

But in a day or so I came to earth and began learning about
the course. I knew all about it on paper, but there is a vast
difference between reading and riding. What a state it was
in! The first seven miles from Douglas to Ballacraine were
of tarmacadam, but the remaining 30 miles, except for a few
hundred yards here and there in villages, had no vestige of
tar in their composition. From Ballacraine onwards it was
one undulating, tortuous course of pure macadam roads—
i.e., earth and stones squeezed together by steam-rollers—
which were deep in dust or treacherous with slime according
to the weather. And the rutted mountain road was grass-
grown in the centre and littered with loose stones. I covered

my first practice lap in just over the hour and thought I had done well.

Gradually, however, my times improved and, along with the others, we were lapping at somewhere about the previous year's speeds—52 to 53 minutes. When one considers the state of the roads, the fact that they were not closed to traffic —horses, cows and sheep, particularly the latter, were frequently encountered—and most of all, the slowness of the machines themselves, this was not bad.

Towards the end of the first week's practising—we had two full weeks in those days—our race machines arrived. They were generally similar to the 1920 models, but had the outside flywheel on the off side. There was a reason for this. On the previous year's machines the normal nearside flywheel half covered the contact breaker, so that accurate magneto timing was difficult, whilst it was almost impossible to adjust the points without removing the flywheel. One of the 1920 riders had had minor contact breaker trouble and had been delayed about half an hour with it, so for 1921 the designers decided to put the flywheel on the other side.

Oh the trouble that caused us! Machines so fitted had performed faultlessly in hill-climbs and speed trials and in tests on the track, but the T.T. course was quite a different matter. Whilst we were running in the engines, all was well, and there was promise of speed far in excess of that of the well-worn practice models. But on the third day on the new models we were given permission to go all out.

Off we set, full of hope of unofficial record laps. All went well for a time, but by about Ramsey I began to feel that things were not so good, and my doubts were confirmed when a 250 New Imperial passed me with ease. I crawled round the Hairpin, foot-slogging heartily to help the tired engine, but at the Gooseneck I was forced to get off and run. Slowly, in bottom gear, I reached the top of the climb.

I have seldom felt more miserable. The hopes of years were shattered—my mount, for my first T.T., was a dud.

Sick at heart I passed the pits and set off for Ballacraine —and the post-mortem on the day's performance. There was only one bright spot, one redeeming feature. I had been the first Levis to start, and I had not been overtaken by a Levis. Obviously the others were in the same boat.

And then I happened to look down at the flywheel, near my right toe. Horror! Instead of a clearly defined flywheel rim there was a horrible furry mass. For a second I thought that the flywheel was loose, but before even I had come to a standstill I knew it was worse than that. As I expected, it was tight enough, but was running over a quarter of an inch out of the true. The crankshaft was bent or distorted!

I must have been the picture of gloom as I stopped at Ballacraine, which was the start and finish of our lap, for I am sure there was a double meaning in Bill Butterfield's " What's the matter, Dave?" He meant not only why had I been so long, but why was my face so long? As I was explaining, the rest of the team crept in, some with my trouble, others with something less serious.

It was a large and gloomy team of directors, riders and mechanics that returned to Peel about six o'clock in the morning—never an hour when one looks too much on the bright side of things. (I have always regretted that I gave up racing before evening practice was introduced). Bill suggested going back to bed, but my mechanic, Harold Wilson, and I were too young and enthusiastic to heed such advice. We hoisted the machine on to its bench forthwith, and before breakfast had the engine stripped.

Everything, apparently, was perfect—yet the flywheel was running out of the true. Bob Newey, the works director who was primarily responsible for the production of the " racers," soon spotted the trouble. It was this:

The crankshaft was of the " three-piece suite " type—the left shaft and balance weight, the right shaft and balance weight and bolted between the two, the roller-bearing big-end assembly. With the driving chain on the left and the fly-wheel on the right the twisting action on the shaft during fierce braking or acceleration was terrific. The big-end nuts were dead tight, but there had been movement between the component parts—very slight movement, of course, but enough to throw the shaft out of true and to tighten up the main bearings. Hence the loss of power I had experienced before Ramsey.

Newey looked glum. He knew those big-end nuts had been tightened properly, but he now tightened each one of them himself, with an enormous spanner. That (we hoped) was that.

Off we set again next day, to return with the same sad story. Mine was the worst, probably because, being the newest member of the team and out to prove myself, I was accelerating and braking more fiercely than the others. Newey looked glummer than ever—the only hope, he said, was to reduce the weight of the flywheel and, consequently, the twisting action caused by momentum and inertia, respectively, during braking and accelerating.

The next thing was to find a lathe—rare things in Peel, and we did not want to take our troubles to Douglas and our bitter enemies, the " New Imps." But I discovered one; it was about 100 years old and large enough to true up a steam-roller flywheel, but it worked. We carved about a pound off the flywheels and returned to reassemble the engines. Next morning I was the only one in trouble, and Newey heaved a sigh of relief. " You'll have to take it easier, Dave," he said. I imagine I looked disgusted, for he went on: " All right, we'll scrape another half pound off it." Which we did.

It did not cure it, although the distortion was not so bad. And, incidentally, with this featherweight flywheel the acceleration was simply terrific—but so must have been the strain on the transmission. Thank heavens it was chain-cum-

of an ordinary engineer's 2-lb. hammer. I did not feel disposed to carry anything heavier; in fact, I bitterly begrudged this extra weight when I was personally riding as light and hard as possible. But it seemed worth while if it would do the job.

It did. The flywheel was out of true as usual after the last morning, but three blows of the lighter hammer put it right. There was only one thing more to complete the apparatus— a simple device for holding up the compression release valve so that I could spin the flywheel to check if it were true. I had by now discovered that, very naturally, the shaft always distorted in the same direction, i.e., the " bouncing spot " on the flywheel was always the same. I marked it with red paint. And after a week-end spent in preparing other parts of the machine I went off to weigh in, hammer and all.

The race itself was my first real motorcycling thrill. The " Flyweights," as they were called, were running with the Juniors, not as a separate class, but all mixed up in one draw for positions. I believe that there were 66 competitors in all, of which one-third were " 250 "; of these there were six Levis riders and five New Imps.

I myself was No. 49, and I was the last of the Levis gang. The others were Albert Milner (Levis favourite) and Bob Pugh, both on all-chain drive models, and " Pa " Applebee, Alan Edwards and Dr. C. H. Hopwood. New Imperials had a strong team, led by Bert Kershaw and Douglas Prentice.

That dreadful period of waiting on the Glencrutchery Road has been described before, but it is a little hard to have to wait until No. 49 in one's first race. However, my turn came at last; the motor started easily and I was soon purring along at speed.

Casualties were heavy in those days and even in the first lap I passed several retired competitors of both Levis and New Imp. camps, besides overtaking other runners. This was good. The flywheel soon showed that it was running slightly out of true, but it did not seem to reduce the speed

—probably the main bearings had got somewhat worn by now, so that the tightening-up effect was not noticeable. Harold Wilson gave me the O.K. sign at the pits and I set off for the second lap in good spirits.

All went well—that was what puzzled me. Lap after lap passing chaps, the roadside littered with abandoned racers, and my machine still going fine. I had seen three Levises retired and had passed two more, so, starting from the back, I was leading my own stable. That cheered me up a lot, particularly as I had also, in one way or another, accounted for all the New Imps. except Doug. Prentice. The flywheel was getting very " furry " in aspect, but " ready rectifier " or no I was out for a non-stop run.

There was frantic excitement amongst the spectators at Ramsey, who were obviously doing some private timing, when I came through on the last lap. Was I really in the running for the Lightweight Cup? Flatter than ever I crouched on the tank, harder I footslogged after the Hairpin and the Gooseneck.

Up the Mountain for the last time, round the Bungalow bend (just), across the tramlines and flat again for the final straight climb. Windy Corner (a near one, that), Keppel Gate (through it somehow), and full bore for Creg-ny-baa. And then, a dreadful roar of engine—broken belt! Brake hard, and haul the machine on to its stand. Legs so cramped and bruised that they give way beneath me. A melange of Levis and self in the middle of the road. Up again, with better luck. Detach spare belt from tummy, push it through pulley and round belt rim. Click—it's on—and off once more.

Oh hell, how much time has been lost? Where's Prentice? Did anyone overtake me as I was wrestling with my model in the roadway? Did the belt fastener break or pull out? Was it due to extra transmission snatch caused by too light a fly-wheel?

I can answer none of those questions except that Prentice was in front and had gained by my misfortune. When I reached the finish my supporters crowded in on me and said " Bad luck, Dave. Lost by two minutes—you're second."

Bad luck? My first race; a newcomer to the team; second! I thought it was fine. I gave the flywheel three sharp blows, just to show it, and repaired to the bar!

So ended my first T.T. race. How much time that belt cost me, and whether or no I should have won if it had held, I can never say. Prentice, some years later, told me that it gave him the race, but I am not so sure. It takes longer to write about falling over a motorcycle than it does to do it. Perhaps—perhaps not. But I was well content, and my stock with the Butterfields and Bob Newey was standing high.

I went back to Luton, Beds., to find my business in a parlous state. One of the firms with whom I had big contracts had gone into liquidation. On the car and motorcycle side it owed me £1,000; on the commercial vehicles I owed it £1,000 (both figures roughly). A normal person such as myself would have thought that all square. " Oh no," said the Official Receiver. " Pay us your £1,000, and we'll pay you a penny or so in the pound on the £1,000 we owe you " or words to that effect.

We were not amused. We trumped that trick by going into liquidation ourselves and left the Official Receiver wondering whether he was playing in Spades or Clubs.

After that painful episode I returned to my native town, Birmingham, and took a job. This got me through the winter, but with the approach of the trials and racing season I became restive. I slipped off one Saturday morning, towards the end of February, 1922, to ride a single-geared Levis in the Colmore Trial, and to win the Levis Cup for the second year in succession.

Back to work again. March. April. Spring was in the air, and entries for the T.T. were rolling in. The first year of a genuine Lightweight Tourist Trophy, as opposed to the Special Cup which had been awarded for " 250 " in the races of 1920 and 1921. I could not keep away.

I went over to Stechford and put my cards on the Butterfields' table. My firm would not allow me to ride in the T.T. Would Butterfields give me a winner for the 1922 Lightweight? " I rode through the Levis field last year," I told them. " I finished second. But for a broken belt I might have won. Will you give me the best you can produce? If you will, I'll throw in my job, and win the 1922 Lightweight for you. Succeed—or Bust."

(S.O.B. the motto: S.O.B. the watchword).

They said they would. Bill Butterfield pretended to hesitate; Arthur Butterfield asked me if I thought it wise. (Wise— with T.T. fire in your blood! Forgive me, Arthur, if you read these lines). Bob Newey nodded and said: " Of course, Dave." Further, they promised to enter me for the French and Belgian Grand Prix races, then second and third in importance in the international calendar.

Into Heaven again! With lying pen I told my firm that I was regretfully terminating my employment with them.

I cut adrift about three weeks before practising started, and haunted the Levis factory from the day of my emancipation until we sailed for the Island. Early on, Bob Newey told me: " I can't give you the speed of the New Imps., or of Wal Handley's O.K. But I can give you nearly the speed, with better acceleration and greater reliability. Get to work on the cycle parts yourself."

I followed his advice with enthusiasm. The factory was preparing six T.T. machines. I was given the run of the works and spent my time in cutting down the weight of my machine. I can say without conceit, I think, that I was the first T.T. rider (or designer, if it comes to that) who realized that ounces count and pounds are invaluable, and acted on the knowledge.

It is surprising how much weight one can save, even without recourse to special-alloy metals. Six machines were being prepared; there were six sets of everything. Starting with the frames and working carefully through every component, even down to such small items as carburetter controls, I weighed six of every single part, and set aside the lightest for myself. Odd as it may seem, everything differs in weight, ever so slightly; by picking the lightest of everything, I saved some 10 lb. By cutting off unnecessary cable lengths, using very narrow handlebars, dispensing with pansy things such as footrest rubbers, shock absorbers, etc., by drilling a bit here and there, by fitting a bicycle saddle—in fact, by weight reduction in every possible way, I saved another 10 lb. When finished, my Levis looked the same as the others, but was 20 lb. lighter. It was three weeks well spent.

I am afraid, however, that I was not too popular with the other Levis riders, who had not had the same opportunities as I. On the other hand, they were all in jobs, and had not so much at stake. Phil Pike (poor old Phil—he was killed in a Plymouth air raid) was particularly sore. "I weigh two stone more than you, Dave," he said; " *I* ought to have the lightest bike." He got quite old-fashioned about it, and we did not really bury the hatchet until some years later, when we became firm friends. But I stuck to my guns—and my bike. S.O.B. the motto.

Harmony was restored when practising began for, as luck would have it, my practice engine was comparatively gutless. The others, with their heavier machines, could leave me easily, and they scoffed accordingly. This was entirely justified, for I had made an infernal nuisance of myself in the factory. But I was not perturbed, for I had Bob Newey's promise that my race engine would be a winner. Fairly patiently, I awaited its arrival.

It came at last, four days before the end of practising. (Bob brought it over himself in a brown paper parcel, under his arm!) It was a lovely, hand-made piece of mechanical

perfection, perfect in workmanship, perfect in design. Harold
Wilson and I fitted it in the machine with loving care. " Run
it in gently," said Bob. " Remember, it's never fired yet."

I did. I covered two laps next morning, and by using an
over-rich mixture, four-stroked all the way. Even so, without any hurry at all, I averaged last year's speed. Fine,
magnificent, marvellous! I could put miles an hour on that.

And then—disaster! We stripped the engine to inspect it
and found everything perfect except that the plug and piston
were " plated " with aluminium. (It was a cast-iron piston,
running with a clearance of 3 thou. at the top and $1\frac{1}{2}$ thou. at
the skirt.) Where had the aluminium come from? The
answer was easy—but horrible. There were aluminium
blocks fitted above each half of the crankcase to raise crankcase compression. The connecting-rod normally cleared
them by about $\frac{1}{8}$ in. on each side. But it had obviously been
bending and scraping the aluminium from them.

Gloom reigned in my quarter of the Levis camp. Most of
the other riders were rather pleased, as was only natural—the
way they said " Bad luck, Dave," was enough to provoke
an assault. Bill and Bob went into conference; I went into
the bar and knocked back a beer while Harold Wilson had a
" lemon." He was loyal enough, but he preferred " lemons "
to beer! Then we went in to hear the verdict.

To-day, 20 years later, I can remember every detail of
that scene. The two of them, sitting on a settee in the empty
billiard room of the Creg Malin Hotel. Two sallow, solemn
faces—two men who had worked for my success harder than
I, and, as manufacturers had even more at stake. Bob said:
" I've cut down the con.-rod too much—not enough H section; but there's no time to get another." Bill said: " Don't
let it four-stroke. Running light like you have puts more
strain on the con.-rod than full throttle. Let her have it to-
morrow, but keep her two-stroking. Four-stroking gives the
con.-rod a fourpenny punch." A long pause. Then Bob
said: " It won't break, Dave. I swear it won't."

Phew! There is no other word to explain my relief. My two gaffers, financial and technical, had guaranteed the engine, and told me to " let her have it." That was all I wanted.

Next day I did as I was told, and lapped (unofficially) in 45½ minutes—about five minutes better than the 1921 average, and, so far as I remember, some three minutes better than that year's record lap. And still some in hand. Stripping the engine revealed no trace of aluminium " scrapings." I had kept her two-stroking and the trouble was cured!

After that we did no more to the engine; it was perfect. We split-pinned, riveted and taped every possible nut and bolt, and had an easy week-end. There was no ribald laughter at the weigh-in, for I had no need of a hammer this time! The flywheel was on the near side again.

There were 32 of us in the Lightweight Race and 48 in the Junior, and the two events were run concurrently. But there was a separate Lightweight Trophy, and the Lightweights all started first—1 to 32 at half-minute intervals. It was a foregone conclusion that the winner would be found amongst the New Imperial, O.K. and Levis stables. Doug. Prentice and Bert Kershaw were the New Imp. stars, Wal. Handley led the O.K. team and Phil Pike, I think, was the Levis favourite. The Velocettes had to be considered, but they were comparative newcomers, whereas the Levis had won the 1920 Lightweight and been second in 1921. But popular rumour said that two-strokes were " finished." I believe the bookies were laying 20 to 1 against me; I wish I had known that before the race. It was not until many years later that I caned the unofficial " bookie " so much that he gave up the unequal struggle and returned to the mainland a poorer but wiser man.

All my life, 11 or any combination of it, has been my lucky number. I had drawn No. 11 for the first genuine Lightweight T.T., and I counted it a good omen.

I set off gently to give the engine a chance, but between Quarter Bridge and Braddan I passed No. 10. Good-o! Now for it. Tucked down clean, I opened the throttle, and my wrist watch (fastened on the forearm, where it is more easily seen in racing) told me that I had reached Ballacraine in good time. Kirkmachael (14 miles) I clocked in 14 minutes dead—not bad for a " 250." But no sign of other riders, except for one or two unfortunates who had already retired.

Then the straight towards Ballaugh. Three chaps approaching it, abreast, and the Bridge looming up ahead. Slow down, and trickle through the village behind them? With Doug. Prentice in front and Wal. Handley behind, tearing towards victory? . . . S.O.B. the motto . . .

Full bore—and now for it! The four of us on the Bridge together, with me, the fastest of them, on the outside—the wrong side for the following right-hand bend. Brake violently, much to their discomfort, and—round!

That won't do—it was asking for it. (" The con.-rod won't break, Dave—I swear it."). Steady does it—Bill and Bob will never forgive me if I crash. But with three passed in one swoop, so to speak, I could reckon on clear running for a few miles. Flat down to it—flatter, you fool!

Sulby—Ramsey—the Gooseneck (no footslogging this year) and then ease back the throttle to save the engine in low and second gears for the mountain climb. A wild, lonely world. Was it all real? Why, why was I tearing along like this, torturing my body and my bike in this mad rush to get round quicker than anyone else? Isolated spectators watched me goofy-eyed and continued with their sandwiches before I had properly passed them. Melancholy mountain sheep stopped grass-cutting for a few seconds to turn soft, languid eyes on me before they resumed their endless task. Fool human, they seemed to say, fool human.

No one who has not been near the front of a T.T. race can explain or understand the unutterable loneliness of the first

lap ascent of Snaefell, or appreciate the feeling of the absurdity of the whole affair that accompanies it. Why, oh why,
was I doing this?

The Bungalow cures it all. Here there is a crowd—and a
cheering crowd, too. Some of them, maybe, have backed
me with the local bookie. Their enthusiasm infects me. I
must be doing well—I am doing well, for what with break-
downs I have already passed six other riders.

Two more slip behind between the Bungalow and the pits.
I started No. 11 and am now third on the road with only No.
1, Doug. Prentice, last year's winner, on a New Imp., and
No. 2, a fellow called Joynson, in front of me. The " O.K."
sign from the pits—i.e., "'you're doing all right, keep it up."

Quarter Bridge again, and on it a rider. Joy! It's Doug.
Prentice, No. 1. Five minutes' gain on last year's winner
in a lap and a mile. And my watch has shown me a lap in
just under 45 minutes, with the record standing at about 48.
Good enough.

Then a long, dull, solitary ride. Bellacraine, Kirkmichael, Sulby—all the usual places. Where's Joynson?
Have I missed him, retired? Who is he, anyway—is he a
dark horse? No, there he is, way up the Mountain, his dust
clearly seen a mile or so ahead. A bit more throttle this
time, and after him, flatter on the tank than ever. Past him
at last, and a clear field.

Keppel—Creg-ny-Baa—Hilberry—Governor's—and so on
past the pits. The " O.K. " sign again from Harold Wilson
and a quick glance showing Bob Newey, imperturbable, but
Bill Butterfield tearing up paper into little bits. Two laps in
under the 1½ hours—slow by modern standards, but almost
unbelievable in those days.

Ballacraine, Kirkmichael, Ramsey again—and there on
the roadside, Wal Handley, disconsolate beside his O.K., but
with a friendly wave all the same. Poor Wal—it was his first
race, and though I didn't know it at the time, he had led on

the first lap, only to retire at Ramsey on the second. But cheerful in adversity, as always.

Back to the pits at last, for replenishments and a bottle of beer—much needed. " You're leading by eight minutes, Dave, take it easy "—Harold Wilson. " But don't let the b—— thing four-stroke!"—this from Bob Newey. A quick fill-up—too quick, as it transpired—and off. And round the whole course again. Why was I doing it, why? Oh, to win the T.T., of course. Of *course*, but what a stupid business.

Eight minutes lead in three laps; Wal Handley and Bert Kershaw out of it; Doug Prentice miles behind. Steady, it's in the bag. Gently does it—*but don't let it four-stroke*. (" The con.-rod won't break, Dave, I swear it.") Keep it two stroking—but take it easy.

Ramsey, the Gooseneck, the Bungalow. Keppel Gate, Creg-ny-Baa, Hilberry. Only one more lap after this, thank heaven. Forty miles from here—but 40 miles of mental and physical torture. (The cycle saddle and my other weight-saving devices were taking their toll).

Have I enough juice? I did three laps on the first tankful; surely, I can do two after replenishing? Still, I'd eight minutes' lead after three laps; it's probably 10 by now. Easy money. Better make sure.

Gently round Governor's Bridge, and off with the filler cap. Horror! About half an inch of petrol only, splashing about. What the——! Who the——? Draw in angrily to my pit.

Follows a brief cussing match about air-locks—and a quick gallon in the tank. (" Ten minutes' lead, Dave—take it easy " . . . . " Keep her two-stroking."). Ballacraine, Kirkmichael, Ballaugh, Sulby, Ramsey—for the last time, thank heaven. Never again on a cycle saddle; never again in dance pumps! Was there ever such pain—feet, hands, wrists, posterior? (Yes, the 1921 Colmore was worse—and this is the T.T. Stick it, you fool.) S.O.B. the motto—

Bungalow, Creg, Hilberry, Governor's—for the last time. A fellow waving a flag—quite a lot of cheering. I've finished

—I must have won! Take the bike off me, chaps—gently now—let's see if I can stand. Easy—yes, I can. Where's that Bar?

"*The winner of the Lightweight race finished very fresh. He had had a comfortable run and had nothing of interest to report . . . .*"—Vide Press.

After the 1922 Lightweight, I rode badly in the Senior Race, and finished 17th. I had been entered by William Watson, who had given me my first chance in an open trial nine years before. But I was never any use on a " 500," although I did not know it until then, and a slow puncture, necessitating two stops per lap for inflation, did not help matters.

Then we all went back to the Mainland and began preparing for the French Grand Prix. Naturally, my engine was stripped and minutely examined, particularly as regards the con.-rod. In spite of the caning it had had in the T.T., there was no further trace of flexing, and once again Bob Newey pronounced: " It won't break, Dave, I swear it." So we decided to use the same rod, and indeed the same machine complete, except for tyres and chains, in the two Continental events.

I had not been in France since five years before, when I had " retired hurt " from that country in the Great War. And what a different country it was! Instead of the mud, blood and stench of the battlefield there were the music, dancing and festivity of Paris, gayest city in the world.

One hectic night finished that phase of the adventure, however, and Harold Wilson and I, with my racer and a spare in the van, were despatched to Strasbourg by M. Lucien Psalty, the French agent for Norton and Levis. To call Lucien a " character " is an understatement. He was (and is) of Greek-Italian parentage, and he spoke medium English at an enormous speed. English, he explained, was one of his worst languages, and he spoke a dozen in all. He could write it perfectly, but in talking his trouble was constant full throttle.

A governor on his tongue would have made him the perfect linguist. As it was, I found that we got on better in French. My own French was slight: (" Donny—moi—deux—bieres," spoken slowly and clearly after considerable preparation, was my best phrase, and a productive one, too), but it got better results than Lucien's spoken English.

The course of the 1922 French Grand Prix was a few miles from the town, and was of the usual triangular type, with two long legs of main road and a connecting section of rather rougher going. It was about 9 miles long, and we Light-weights had to cover 20 laps, so that it was about the same length as the Lightweight T.T., which in those days was of five laps only—$187\frac{1}{2}$ miles. The main difference, apart from the short lap course, was that a massed start was employed.

There was little to do in the way of learning the circuit, and nothing to do on the machine except the usual final preparation, so we enjoyed Strasbourg to the full, day and night. (Alda, Marcelle, I wonder where *you* are now? But wherever you are you must be forty-five-ish, and probably very fat, as all true Stras-bourgeoises!) But we kept clear of the Cabaret Continentale the night before the race . . .

So far as I remember there were about 20 starters in the Lightweight class, but I was not unduly worried about any of them except Bert Kershaw, who was representing the New Imp. stable, and with whom I had quickly formed a close friendship. Stanley Woods was one of my rivals, but he was small beer in those days—little we knew of the future!

After much shouting and gesticulating we were all lined up in the road. Then a perfect crescendo of shouting and waving, and, finally, just when we were not expecting it, the signal to start, so that we nearly fell over our machines and each other in our efforts to urge silent engines into song.

Psalty had specially warned me against a pair of riders who were the X—— company's appointed " chuckers off." It had taken him an hour to impart this information at about 6,800 r.p.m., and had necessitated much use of a dictionary

and the back of an envelope. But there it was. This firm
had entered two tough-eggs for the set purpose of crashing
us—Continental sport in 1922! I passed on the news to Bert
and the others, and if the chuckers-off tried any tricks they
got as good as they gave.

After a bit we all got away and began to pick gaps in the
crowd. I was near the front of the 250's and as we thinned
out on the approach to the first hairpin I knew I was running
fourth. That was all right; there was a long way to go and
I was certain of my machine, which is more than could be
said of most of the others.

It was a remarkable race, that French Grand Prix. Never,
except in the 1923 Belgian, have I ridden so hard; never, in
any race, have I won so easily. I rode flat out all the way,
which I had not done even in the T.T., and I won by over
25 minutes! This is what happened.

Once round the first hair-pin I spotted a couple of 250's
ahead and gave chase. Slowly but steadily I overhauled
them and so knew I must be lying second to Kershaw. My
pit showed me no signal for the first few laps, but I knew
Kershaw was ahead and gave the model all it would take.
After a bit, my pit showed the O.K. sign, but I refused to
play. Bert, my friend and enemy, was ahead and I was full
bore after him. S.O.B.

Then the pit gave me the " flat out." " Well, I know
that," thought I, sarcastically. And flat out I continued.

Lap 10—in I came for juice. " Where's Kershaw?" I
yelled. " Kershaw?" they scoffed. " Oh, he retired ages
ago. It's Jim Whalley, on the Massey-Arran. He's only just
behind you. Here he is coming in for a fill-up now. He's
been gaining on you. Go like blazes " (only they didn't say
" blazes ").

Oh, so it was Jim Whalley this time! We had never even
considered him seriously. That fine ride of his in the 1921
Junior T.T. was a flash in the pan, we had said. But here he
was, hot on my track and overtaking me. Hell's bells!

Off once more, full throttle, elbows tucked in, head under handlebars. Jim Whalley, indeed. Vivid recollections of how he had nearly shown the A.J.S. camp the way in last year's Junior. Was he going to show the Levis camp to-day? Round after the eleventh lap and no sign from the pits. Taking stock, of course—they won't know till he comes past —I'll get the signal next time. Jim Whalley with his Massey-Arran-Blackburne; what a mouthful—but what a combination!

Lap 12, the flat out sign; lap 13, ditto; laps 14, 15, 16, 17 and 18, ditto. Lap 19, " flat-out-issimo," with Psalty hopping up and down in the pit like a galvanized Jack-in-the-Box. A nightmare, this, unable to look back and see how far behind he is—like running terrified down a dark corridor with some dreadful spectre overtaking one, ready to strike.

The last hairpin, the last rough stretch, the last straight, the finish. Psalty's embraces, and many others, too, mostly bearded. " Where's Whalley?" " Just behind, deux seconds toujours . . . " " Two seconds my foot, I've been here three minutes," and so on. The second man (I forget who he was) toured in 26 minutes later, and Jim ambled along after about an hour, having broken down on the last lap. For 170 miles he had been within about 200 yards of me and except during the pit stop I had never seen him. A curious race . . .

" Bieres, bieres, beaucoup de bieres. What, champagne? It's a bit early pour le champagne, isn't it, Psalty, mon vieux? Ah well, if you insist . . . " The Cabaret Continentale, evening. " Bon soir, Alda, bon soir, Marcelle. Oui, j'ai gagné. Pauvre Monsieur Bert est cassé as to some of the twiddly bits. You never could trust those quatre-tempts moteurs, compris? Garcon, la carte des vins. Comment, Marcelle, champagne? You'll cost me all my winnings!" Champagne, champagne—toujours la champagne . . . "

So ended the French Grand Prix, and after a day in bed to recover from the stiffness and the Cabaret Continentale, we set off to another lovely place, Spa, in the Ardennes, for the " Belgian."

We found Spa a most pleasant town, more conducive to hard training than Strasbourg, with its many counter attractions. And having acquired a lock-up stable attached to the Hotel Brittanique, famous as German G.H.Q. during the previous war, Harold Wilson and I set about dismantling the engine. On detaching the piston an elusive circlip sprang out of my fingers, and as we could not find it anywhere amongst the straw—talk about looking for a needle in a haystack!—we decided that it must have popped down the crankcase. Cursing heartily, for it was very hot and we felt most unlike work, we dismantled the engine. We found no circlip, of course, but we did find that one of the main roller bearings had seized up solid and was whizzing round, en bloc, in the aluminium. The good gods must have been looking after me in 1922!

We obtained and fitted a new bearing and I set off to learn the course. What a course it was in those days! Ten miles odd of hairpins, twists and turns, with sharp hills and long, sweeping descents. Ten miles odd of stone and earth roads, running through beautiful woods which, to the racing motorcyclist, spelt disaster at every turn. A tricky course, that needed a lot of learning and a greater degree of endurance than even the T.T. itself.

We practised at all times of the day, in blazing weather, and I, personally, had no trouble at all. The bike was " right "; and after a few days I told myself that I knew the course. Harold, Bert Kershaw and I luxuriated in the Hotel Brittanique, and wondered if General Ludendorff had sat in the same chairs and fed off the same tables. Three years, almost to a day, since the signing of the Great Peace—it was pleasant to be honoured visitors in the fine hotel which poor over-run Belgium had sacrificed to the German High Command. Dirty as we were at most times—and it must be admitted that the maitre d'hotel often regarded us askance

—we felt that we were more welcome than our war-time pre-
decessors.

With a leisurely practice period and no Cabaret Continentale to turn night into day, I was fighting fit for the
Sunday of the Grand Prix de Belgique—which was just as
well. There was a mighty hubbub in Spa from about 4 a.m.
onwards, and with typical Belgian thoroughness the roads
were closed to all traffic so early that most of the competitors
had great difficulty in reaching the start. But you cannot
ring up the curtain if none of the actors are there, and after
protracted arguments and much gesticulation we were allowed
to take our places on the stage.

Up went the curtain—and, almost immediately, down came
the rain. How it rained! Despite my T.T. vows, my racing
kit was as before: dance pumps, light stockings, drill breeches
(held in by garters to reduce windage), cricket sweater,
wash-leather gloves—and a crash hat; nothing else at all.
And, though I did not know it, I was setting off for a race
through a four-hour thunderstorm!

Gone the warmth and beauty of the Ardennes. Instead,
black clouds, thunder and lightning, with grey sheets of lash-
ing rain. I was soaked to the skin in a hundred yards—and
I had 200 miles to go.

On I went, slithering over mud-bound roads, sluicing
through lake-puddles, skidding this way and that, swearing
incessantly at the misery, futility and absurdity of the whole
proceeding, a 50 m.p.h. human sponge, with water pouring
from chin, hands, elbows, heels. What a fool game! Was
it worth it? Was anything worth this agony of cold? Why,
oh why, was I doing it?

So through the hours, we surged our way. My own passage
was halted every 30 to 40 miles by the need of a new sparking plug. I had had no trouble of this sort in previous races
and could not understand it, until, sheltered by the kindly
umbrella of a Belgian spectator, I glanced at the cylinder. It
was coated with the mud through which we swirled, baked

hard on to it. Heat radiation was practically non-existent—no wonder the plug took a poor view!

Each time I stopped, Walter Handley, on his 250 O.K., cascaded past me laughing in his misery, as usual. Each time I got going I passed him at the roadside, coaxing water out of his magneto. A wave of the hand, and on through the solid sheets of rain.

At 10 laps I stopped for petrol. Harold Wilson, God bless him, had got my customary mid-race bottle of beer ready according to instructions, but he had exceeded his instructions, by gathering a small bottle of " cognac," too, in case I had changed my mind in the matter of stimulants. Had I not! Beer would have frozen on the way down; cognac could almost thaw the corpse.

While Harold was filling the tank, I set to with a will, but before I had half finished the bottle Dougal Marchant, Handley's manager, jumped from the adjacent pit and knocked the bottle from my frozen fingers. It was the most sporting action in the world, for Walter and I (although I did not know it) were the only ones with any chance of winning, and an overdose of cognac might easily have put me out. But I cursed him at the time! Dougal did not know the strength of my head, nor, from the shelter of his pit, the terrible coldness of my body. I believe that I could have swallowed all that firewater and continued without misjudging a bend.

As it was, what I had did me a lot of good, and I was not entirely miserable for the next two laps. Now and again I passed Walter, drying his magneto; now and again Walter passed me changing a plug. I had seen Bert Kershaw padding his way home with water spouting from his elbows and the seat of his trousers as if someone had left the taps turned on. Every now and then Alec Jackson, leading in the Senior race on his Sunbeam, splashed past me; for several laps I rode alongside Remington, the Junior leader, and together we clapped our arms, cabman fashion, in a vain attempt to restore circulation. And still the rain fell in grey, solid sheets.

Odd snatches from the Bible, adapted to the circumstances, kept running through my head: " What shall it profit a man if he win two races and lose his life from pneumonia in the third?" If it had not been for Handley I would have stopped and finished off that cognac—unless Dougal had already finished it! Still, there were only 50 more miles to go.

And so at last that dreadful race ended. Within three miles of the finish, on the climb from Stavelot to Francorchamps, I fitted the last of my spare plugs in sodden terror that Handley would come spraying past and rob me of victory on the post. But no, he was dealing with his own troubles on the far side of the course. With numbed limbs I forced my tired engine into life, fell on to the tank, splashed my way round the Francorchamps hairpin for the last time and tumbled off the machine by my pit. Had I won! I was scarcely interested—what did it matter. Cognac, cognac!

But little cognac for me! Twenty bearded kisses (for it seemed that I had won) and then a muscular bloke, " Dunlop " Buckley, harried and carried me to an adjacent cottage where, bless him, too, he had provided a hip bath and several buckets of boiling water. How they scalded me, how they tore the skin off me as they wrenched hot, coarse towels across my tender shoulders and back. But, probably, they saved my life, for if anyone had courted pneumonia, I had, with little more than a swim-suit as clothing for a four-hour thunderstorm.

The buffet at last, clad in the Belgian cottager's Sunday-best, which he sold me for the modest sum of 40 francs. Look after the bike, Harold, I'm all in. The luxurious warmth and comfort of the Hotel Brittanique. More cognac. No, pas de diner, merci. The T.T., the French Grand Prix, the Belgian —the Hat Trick! But what does it profit a man? . . . Bed, bed—blissful, horizontal warmth; wonderful clouds of sleep; the Hat Trick—nice, yes, quite nice, but warmth, peace, sleep, utter oblivion. These are worth more than Hat Tricks.

So ended the 1922 racing season, so far as I was concerned.
I had good reason to be satisfied with the result and with my
" S.O.B. " decision of the months before. Now for a few
trials and a peaceful winter.

Every dog has his day—and every racing motorcyclist
his lucky season. Mine was 1922, and surely I could
ask no more. To have won the three big races for the
first time by any rider in any class was an achievement of
which, 20 years later, I am still proud—justifiably, I think.
The credit for this was due mainly to the Levis engineers
and, in particular, to Bob Newey, designer and actual personal manufacturer of that " very remarkable two-stroke
engine." That engine, by the way, passed out completely
after the 1922 Belgian G.P. When we took the pot off at the
final examination the piston rings, worn to paper thinness by
the stream of abrasive mud which for four hours had poured
in through my voracious carburetter, sprang off the piston
and crumpled to dust in our fingers as we tried to refit them.
The cylinder was also so worn that a rebore would have made
it oversize. So, after I stopped it at the pits of Francorchamps, that wonderful, perfect engine never fired again.
But had it not done its stuff? I had no complaints.

My luck still held in the two big trials that followed—the
A.-C.U. Six Days and the " International "—in the latter
particularly. This event was being held in Switzerland, the
Swiss team having won it the previous year, and the A.-C.U.
had selected the three T.T. winners—Alec Bennett, Tom
Sheard and I—as the British team. Rumour had it that Tom
Sheard had never left his native Isle of Man and did not pro-
pose to risk his life on the high seas to ride in a footling event
like the International Six Days Trial. His place was taken
by Frank Giles, with an A.J.S. combination, whilst Alec and
I rode solo, Sunbeam and Levis respectively.

The British team lost—by one mark—but I had no personal reason for reproach, for my little fizz-box took me to

the finish with 1,000 marks out of 1,000, which included the final examination—an inspection far more rigorous than any Army " 406." Unfortunately, Frank lost four marks in the timed hill-climb—he was on an 800 c.c. model, competing on equal terms with the 1000's. When we finished the course at Geneva, we had lost four marks against the Swiss team's 10, so we seemed to be sitting pretty. But the officials penalized Alec six marks for a broken saddle spring or bracket— the maximum penalty for a broken frame—which put the teams level, and then, on a further examination, docked him the final, decisive point for a faint oil leak on one of the many oil pipes of Sunbeams of the period.

Having thereby won for themselves the Trophy, the Swiss officials showered awards upon us. I myself collected a medaille d'or, a grande medaille d'or, two silver cups and, best of all, a magnificent 18 carat gold hunter watch, presented by the Geneva police. I have always treasured this, for those same Geneva police nearly prevented me from riding in the event at all. The night before the official weigh-in I became involved in a cabaret affair and found, to my dismay, that in such cases the Swiss police held views less tolerant than those of the French and Belgian gendarmes. They let me out in the morning, however, somewhat poorer one way and another, just in time to gather the model and present myself. Poor Mr. Loughborough was most worried!

The sun had set on the 1922 season, and I resigned myself to an office chair until the Colmore Cup Trial brought the dawn of 1923. I was pleased with my machine in that event, for it not only won me the Levis Cup for the third (and last) year in succession, but carried me successfully through a stop-and re-start test on the 1 in $4\frac{1}{2}$ gradient of Rising Sun. As the machine was single-geared and clutchless there was some comment on this performance, but the procedure was really simple. On my arrival between the stop-and-re-start tapes, I stopped the engine and yanked the model on to its stand. I then restarted the engine by pulling the back wheel and took my seat. On the word " Go " I gave her full throttle and pushed her off the stand. Wheelspin provided a clutch effect and I just petered over the top. Yet many three-speeders failed!

Trials were fun, particularly the Travers, which I was lucky enough to win on a Levis with an " occasional water-cooling system " of my own natural design. But the races were the real game. I was entered for the same three events—T.T., French and Belgian—and I looked forward optimistically to repeating my 1922 successes.

I think I am right in saying that in those days no rider had ever won two T.T. races in succession, and I was certainly not of the class to do it—it is only the Bennetts, the Handleys and the Woods and the Guthries who can claim such honours. Moreover, my race engine, hand-made by Bob Newey as before, was not finished until two days after the race! So that was that. I used my practice engine and finished just within Replica time after a rather harrowing ride. It was just as well that I did not waste a good engine on it, for one of the bottom fork links broke and I rode the last lap with the front wheel meandering away from the machine, expecting at any moment to be decanted on my chin in the roadway. And all for a replica and the scanty " boni " thereof!

Bob was apologetic about the engine, but we looked on the bright side and set off for the French Grand Prix in high hope. In sharp contrast to the previous year's event, when I went full bore throughout with Jim Whalley on my track, this was the easiest ride I have ever had. It was run off on the Tours circuit and my only serious competitors were Len Horton (New Imperial) and Paddy Johnson (Cotton). Len broke down in the first lap and Paddy was lacking in knots. I pottered round on half-throttle and won by some 10 minutes at about 55 m.p.h.—two or three m.p.h. faster than in the 1922 event when I had gone flat out on a similar circuit. That engine was as remarkable in its way as the 1922 one, but less spectacular.

No two races are the same, and each is usually quite different from its predecessor. Just as the French had been different, so was the Belgian. In 1922, an easy win (on time) after the most dreadful race in history, with Wal. Handley, my only real competitor, in even more trouble than me. In 1923, Walter again, on a faster and more reliable machine . . . For 18 laps we roared round, side by side, outstripping the field, and, though we were on Lightweights, making all the Juniors and most of the Seniors look like also-rans. With a lap and a half to go, Walter waved me good-bye and raced off by himself, to beat me by a couple of minutes. Some idea of the scrap we had and the speed we set may be gathered from the fact that Walter and I, on Lightweights, were second and third fastest of the day, beating everyone except Freddie Dixon, the winner of the Senior event.

So the racing calendar went on. " Every dog has his day." My star was falling. It was not so much that I was " past racing " as that the straightforward, cast-iron piston two-stroke was past it. The twiddly bits of the four-strokes had ceased to disintegrate, and as four-strokes had always been faster, the days of the racing " 250 " two-stroke were obviously numbered. I came down in the world—to the " 175 " class for the 1924 season, and won the Belgian " Ultra-Lightweight "; but apart from that I had to be content with a third in the French G.P. and a fourth in the 175 c.c. T.T.—of massed start fame.

Then Bill Butterfield told me regretfully that Levises were giving up racing, so in 1925 I got married instead and, as is customary in the holy estate of matrimony, proceeded to " settle down." Or so I thought!

Before I pass to other things—and my tale is nearing its end—I must pay tribute to the Levis firm. In the years 1921 to 1924 they provided me with machines for twelve major races, five T.T. and seven Continental. Every single Levis carried me to the finish which, in a round dozen of races, is, I should imagine, a record which even Stanley Woods cannot beat. In those twelve races I had five firsts, two seconds, two thirds, a fourth and two T.T. replicas—not too bad a score on points. And all on a perfectly simple three-port two-stroke engine with a cast-iron piston and nothing special at all— except workmanship. All credit to the Butterfield brothers, Bob Newey, Alan Edwards, Harold Wilson and others, who worked long hours into the night making those perfectly simple engines simply perfect.

Married and settled down—was ever such a contradiction in terms? We certainly meant to settle down, but we started with a Winter Sports honeymoon, in January, 1925, and the excitement and mild risks of that adventure must have got into our blood. We tried hard, but we were fighting a losing battle.

Part of the settling-down process was that I gave up racing and was proud to get a job again on the staff of " Motor Cycling," this time as chief editorial man and occasional editor. I pointed out to the management that my talents fitted me for outside work, reporting all the big events, and so on. This, I thought, would satisfy my enthusiasm for motorcycling sport and yet would be in keeping with the " settling-down " business.

It worked for about four months, but in May the T.T. bug got me again. There was no hope of competing, but could I get a bit of riding? " Long I pondered o'er the question "— in my Douglas boarding house. Then I sent the firm an eight-shilling telegram (the firm paid!) suggesting that I should do some practice laps on a Lightweight, a Junior and a Senior machine, and write a " road test " article on T.T. machines on the T.T. course. I spent about three shillings in explaining that I was probably the only journalist in the world to whom the firms would trust their T.T. models, and that it was a scoop—as it undoubtedly was. Dear Firm wired back " Yes " at a cost of sixpence, and off I went again. I arranged to borrow a Lightweight New Imp., a Junior Sun-beam and a Scott. With the playful connivance of the

A.-C.U., I became " K " reserve, under the unusual but descriptive nom-de-course of " Ferodo Vaselini."

In 1925 there had been rumours of the " Italian invasion " of the Island, which in fact, took place the next year, but they were rumours only. So the arrival of a real live ice-cream vendor (the term "Wop" had not then been invented, of course) created a stir.

Actually, my first lap as " Ferodo " was far more exciting for me than for the crowd. I started on a Scott, having stayed overnight at the Scott headquarters in Ramsey. In the early light I smeared my cheeks and chin with burnt cork, to give the appearance of Southern swarthiness, and affixed an immense black moustache to my upper lip. The Dunlop man and policeman in Parliament Square nearly had heart failure when I appeared from a side road, but I was past them before they recovered, and away towards the Hairpin. Here the spectators got another shock, for just as a dark-skinned apparition approached them, a side-wind caught its moustache and revealed a very pink English upper lip. Realizing that part of my disguise had gone, I rubbed the burnt cork from my chin and cheeks all over my face—nose as well, by mistake—and continued at speed. Towards the end of the climb, the model lost a cylinder. Not wanting to stop on the gradient, I continued on one, but just before the Bungalow bend I happened to glance down, and was horrified to find that the motor was on fire beneath me. Thinking very quickly, I shut off the petrol, turned right at The Bungalow, down the Sulby Glen road, knocked the gear into neutral, shoved my feet on the handlebars, and coasted down the hill, relying on the wind to keep the flames from the tank and petrol pipes. This worked perfectly, for everything that could burn—H.T. wires, and so on—had burnt itself out by the time I reached Sulby Glen Hotel, and the damage, although it looked extensive, could have been reckoned in shillings.

I was a little proud of myself, for had I stopped at the first sign of fire (it was caused, of course, by an H.T. lead jumping off and sparking against the carburettor) the model would have been a complete write-off. I was surprised, however, by the solicitude of the officials and spectators at the Glen, who assumed that the state of my face was connected with the conflagration, and pressed flasks on me, which I grate-fully accepted. They were somewhat annoyed, I am afraid, when I explained that my " complexion " was merely a whim, and seemed to begrudge the whisky! But I felt I had deserved it.

After that I had non-stop runs on each of my T.T. mounts, and wrote an article for " Motor Cycling " which was at least the first of its kind.

Marry and settle down! Of all unsettling things, the T.T. is the worst, or best. My wife, who had hitherto regarded motorcycles as things on the right side of sidecars, or as vehicles which blew her to pieces when she rode on the back of them (" Here, tie a cushion on, quick, we're off!") found herself in a new, wild world, where Alec Bennett, Howard Davies and Wal Handley were the gods who counted. Settle down, indeed! Far from settling down, she was doomed to a life of anxiety and adventure; and has not regretted it.

In the spring of 1926, the T.T. bug attacked me again, this time in so virulent a form that I succumbed to it. The management of " Motor Cycling " naturally could not allow its staff weeks off to compete in the T.T. and the Continental events. So, regretfully, we parted company. In the four seasons that followed I rode various makes—New Imperials, Rex-Acmes, Levis and Velocette, but my star was falling. I collected a few seconds and thirds, but never again a laurel wreath or the bearded Continental kisses. And in 1929 I packed it in for good.

Marry and settle down! The T.T. bug, once in your sys-tem, is not easily expelled. You may tell yourself that you have finished racing, and you may be true in saying so. You may sit back, drive about in motorcars, and try to settle down. But all the time the microbes are breeding, massing for the attack. Sometimes the disease shows itself in no worse a form than the use of queer, costly motorcars, such as 30-98 Vauxhalls, 4½-litre Bentleys and the like; sometimes it leads one to adventures in new fields.

In my own case, it introduced me to motor boats and aeroplanes, in that order. By motor boats I do not mean the small craft that chuff about rivers and harbours, but real, heman, sea-going craft. I bought a fine 50-ft. ship, giving a Bentley car (earlier symptom of the disease) in part exchange. In 1931 I took it for a short sea cruise, and in 1932 I sailed it from Worcester to the Isle of Man—a distance of nearly 400 miles—starting four up and finishing with two only —Bob Holliday, well-known to " Motor Cycling " readers, and myself.

The T.T. bug should have been satisfied. for during those two trips we had more than our fill of adventures. For example: (a) we sank a vast ferry boat and won the ensuing County Court case; (b) smashed our own propeller shaft and mended it with a pair of Levis front axles from the junk box; (c) broke our mast against the over-hanging dinghy of . a lightship which wanted us to collect its letters; (d) broke our rudder on some hidden rocks off the Pembroke coast; (e) made a new one in Fishguard from a piece of factory shafting and a Dunlop tyre sign; (f) steered by the North Star from Fishguard to Anglesey and by the sun onwards, the compass having packed up, and (g) reached the Isle of Man. Did ever T.T. races provide so much excitement?

But the microbe was not satisfied and soon it had me flying. In this adventure, as on later boat cruises, when she was appointed ship's doctor and quartermistress, my wife accompanied me, and, having qualified for our " A " licences, we gained our real knowledge of air " craft " and navigation from Wal. Handley, one of the finest pilots I have ever known. He was superb in the air, just as he was unrivalled on two wheels or four.

Time creeps on—1936, '37, '38. Twice in a week the aeroplane I was unlucky enough to own nearly killed Walter and me, with its sudden engine failures. " Never again in *that* " said Walter. A year later my wife and I gave up flying; Walter continued, with the tragic end we know.

My tale draws to its close. War—my second war. Back to the Army again in my old job. Getting on—ten or twelve years older than the Boer War " dug-outs " who had seemed to me so antique in the war-to-end-war. But perhaps the T.T. bug keeps one young.

Back to the Army—and back to motorcycles. No longer are motorcycles considered " dirty, noisy things that should be suppressed by law." They may be noisy, despatch riders may be dirty. But without them where would we be?

The T.T. bug again, but in a new war-time guise. No speed this time—40 m.p.h. limit enforced ruthlessly by the C.M.P., speed cops of to-day, as yesterday. But scrambles, the roughest of rough stuff, " impossible " acclivities and descents, Scott-trial water-splashes. A couple of personal acquisitions, a " 350 " Empire Star and a " 500 " Red Hunter . . .

Aeroplane sold, thank heavens; boat in dry dock; car laid up for the duration. But still I have my Army Nortons and my D.R. training. The T.T. bug is satisfied . . . For a time.

I began this tale in October; it is now December, and the motorcycle " basic " has gone. The Red Hunter is laid up at my home; to-day, sorrowfully and criminally, I rode the Beeza to the railway station, with a label on its handlebars. The tram lines were in that treacherous state which so often caused the De Dion to throw me from it forty years ago . . .

Two fat policemen on bicycles bar the fairway. I have no business on the road at all. Try to sneak past without crossing the murderous tramlines; fail. A whirr of sparks, and I pile up in a heap before them. A very decent box of tacks. Forty years on—

So history repeats itself.

INDEX

N/KEN/1

KENSINGTON · PUBLIC · LIBRARIES

am

15-11-48

19
1